To Bob,
With best wishes,
P.R. Hale
9/6/99
2

FLAT CAPS AND BICYCLE CLIPS

A HISTORY OF
LINDRICK ARTISANS GOLF CLUB
1899 – 1999

PETER R HALL

Dedication

This book is dedicated to the memory of
Alice Barclay Morris.
1922-1996

Published by:
Engage Enterprises Limited
Westwoods, Worksop Road, Woodsetts, Worksop,
Nottinghamshire S81 8AN

© 1999 Peter R Hall

The rights of All rights reserved. No part of this publication may be reproduced, stored in a retrieval system, or be transmitted in any form or by any means, electronic, mechanical, photocopying, recording or otherwise without the prior permission of Peter R Hall

Printed and bound by:
MFP Design & Print, Stretford, Manchester M32 0JT

ACKNOWLEDGEMENTS

This book could not have been written without the assistance of many people. I am indebted to Andrew C. Booth, whose patience I tested on many occasions when attempting to learn a new computer routine, and whose invaluable help enabled me to pull this work together.

The assistance given by Susan Woods, Chief Librarian at Sheffield Newspapers, who gave her services with enthusiasm, particularly in extracting archive information buried in the bowels of the newspaper, provided me with an insight in to the club's long past that was most beneficial. Worksop Public Library performed a similar role with equal aplomb, and I am indebted to them also.

My thanks also go to Tony Everett of the Artisan Golfers Association, whose archive of Artisan material proved to be so rewarding, as well as that of the Northern Section Secretary, Frank Brookhouse.

I am grateful to the members of the Lindrick Artisans Golf Club, both past and present, who cheerfully gave their time to pass on their memories, whilst having to endure my repeated questioning. In particular I would like to thank Roy Kipling for his generous support and encouragement. His vast knowledge, not just of Lindrick Artisans Golf Club, but of Artisan golf in general, proved time and again invaluable in the research process for this work. Both Roy and Ellis Colton assisted in the proof reading, and I am indebted to them for their guidance in this matter.

Also I would like to acknowledge the assistance given by Lindrick Golf Club, in particular the Secretary, Lieutenant-Commander Robin Jack, whilst also thanking them for all that we enjoy.

Finally, my thanks go to my wife Carol, who has endured my determination to complete this work on time, and who from time to time has encouraged me through the most tedious aspects of this project.

Without the help of all of these people this book could not have been written.

FOREWORD

It is now one hundred years since the Artisans of Woodsetts, Shireoaks and Turnerwood were allowed the privilege of playing golf at Lindrick by the members of the Sheffield and District Golf Club. Since May 9th 1899 many great golfing events have occurred at Lindrick, many of which have involved the Artisans. So much so, that in 1979, J. Arthur-Colver wrote, in his *History of Lindrick Golf Club*, that; "possibly a history of the Artisans will be written by one of their members depicting golf at Lindrick as seen purely within the local environment".

This book is an attempt to tell something of that history.

As the millennium draws ever more quickly upon us, it is hard to believe that the pioneers of Artisan golf would leave us a legacy which we still enjoy today, but their enthusiasm: playing golf with clubs made from roots and wooden balls, has cascaded down the decades as each new generation has taken up the responsibility of moving the club forward. The Artisans of Lindrick, one of the first such clubs in England, have not only produced some great players over the years: names such as Taylor, Rowett, Colton, Merrick, Waterhouse, Widdison and Spencer have always been synonymous with this, but also in the administration and politics of the Artisan movement as a whole.

Jack Clarkson should be mentioned in particular. Secretary from 1930 to 1978, Jack was "Artisan Golf" at Lindrick. His re-building of the club after W.W II is a testament to his boundless energy and gritty determination. By 1960, Lindrick Artisans had a club and clubhouse that was the envy of the country and on reflection, this represented the pinnacle of his Artisan career. In addition, Jack was also Chairman of the Northern Section of the Artisan Golfers Association, where he wielded great influence over many years.

Nevertheless, others have been equally devoted to the club. Names such as Sam Herrington, Treasurer, Tom Neal, Secretary, Harry Goacher, Chairman, R. O. Spencer, also Chairman, Leonard Kipling, Match Secretary, Roy Kipling, also Match Secretary and Secretary, Arnold Knowles, Treasurer, Ellis Colton, also Treasurer, and Eric

Taylor, Match Secretary, have given nothing less than total commitment during their periods of official office. This is not to say that these people have looked after the affairs of the club by themselves. Far from it. Over the one hundred years of the club scores of others have freely given their time as committeemen and volunteered for various other duties that have been greatly appreciated by all concerned. To mention them all by name would be a book in itself; suffice to say everyone has contributed at some point.

The other great office of the club is that of the President, and this man has always been a senior member of the Parent Club. Down the years the Artisans have been blessed by Presidents who have not just been sympathetic to the club, but also visionary in their outlook. At the same time they have been supported by equally enthusiastic Vice Presidents. Many of the Clubs prize's and cup's bear the names of these benefactors. Two Presidents stand out in the history of the Club, these being George Denton, who formalised the re-structure of the Club in 1912 and Jack Ridgway, whose financial support in the 1950's helped in re-building the clubhouse. Again, at some point all the Presidents have been influential in one way or another.

It is difficult to imagine what the club was like in the early days, but from the beginning progress was made steadily. There is no record of any clubhouse facilities in 1899, but by 1919 this had been established in its present location. The golf played was very competitive, names such as Harry Goacher, Ted Highfield, Arnold Cawkwell and his brother Horace, along with Arnold and Frank Taylor being the dominant forces. By the 1920's and '30's the balance of power had changed. Play now being dominated by Horace Merrick, Cliff Herrington and Charlie Colton.

The Second World War disrupted proceedings but afterwards a new generation came to the fore, players such as Bill Randall, Ellis Colton, Jim Waterhouse, Norman Tyson, Alan Spencer, Roy Rowett and Jim Merrick. These were halcyon days as the Artisans started to spread their wings and capture prizes and trophies at the Northern Artisan Tournament. The golfing reputation of the club grew, and anyone who was up against the Artisans knew they were in for a tough match.

In the 1960's and '70's corporate sponsored club events came in to being and play was now dominated by Clive Betts, Roy Kipling, Alan Taylor, Derek Waterhouse and Ken Widdison. At the same time the Ryder Cup, which had been won in 1957, and other sponsored events, such as the Dunlop Masters and Sun Alliance Matchplay Championship were played. These professional events allowed the Artisans to contribute as caddies, stewards and course helpers. Jobs that were accomplished with assurance.

The early 1980's were a transitional period, as the club down sized from 70 male and 20 female members to its current form of 60 total members. Not unnaturally, this caused much bad feeling between the Artisans and the Parent Club. This was unfortunate, as this was the first time any significant friction had existed between the clubs since the early 1920's. Matches with the Parent Club had been in existence from at least 1914 and these had always been played in the best of spirits. Fortunately good sense prevailed, and within a short period of time relations had stabilised and it was possible once again to look to the future. During this time a new group of players emerged, men such as Roger Merrick, David Locke, Mark Merrick and David Rowett.

The history of the club can not be told without discussing the Ladies section, which was formed in 1924. They have over the years made a great contribution to the Club and have their own story to tell which can be read in later chapters, but names such as Vivian Jacobs, Janet Twibell and Gwen Steadman stand out as influential characters down the years. In modern times the ladies section has declined badly and only time will tell if it still has a future. Hopefully it will.

This book is about all of these things and many more. It is, above all, a book about the members, their exploits and ultimately their achievements.

TABLE OF CONTENTS

FOREWORD	4
TABLE OF CONTENTS	6
PART 1	9
CHAPTER 1 IN THE BEGINNING	10
CHAPTER 2 A GAME OF THEIR OWN 1899 – 1912	12
CHAPTER 3 THE CALM AND THE STORM 1912 – 1918	14
CHAPTER 4 THE TWENTY'S 1919 – 1930	17
CHAPTER 5 TEAM MATCHES 1912 – 1939	23
CHAPTER 6 CLUB BUSINESS 1924 – 1939	27
CHAPTER 7 GOLF IN THE 30's 1930 – 1939	33
CHAPTER 8 CLUBHOUSE DEVELOPMENTS 1919 – 1939	38
CHAPTER 9 LADY ARTISAN GOLFERS 1913 – 1939	42
CHAPTER 10 ARTISANS AT WAR 1939 – 1945	46
PART 2	51
CHAPTER 11 SORTING OUT THE MESS 1946 – 1951	52
CHAPTER 12 GOLF IN THE 50's	57
CHAPTER 13 CLUB AFFAIRS 1946 – 70	61
CHAPTER 14 A CLUB TO RIVAL ALL OTHERS 1951 – 1962	68
CHAPTER 15 THE SWINGING 60's AND THE GLAMOROUS 70's	72
CHAPTER 16 THE NORTHERN SECTION TOURNAMENT 1946 – 1998	80
CHAPTER 17 UPSETTING THE APPLECART 1978 – 1980	88
CHAPTER 18 THE IRISH QUESTION 1970 – 1999	95
CHAPTER 19 LINDRICK ON THE BIG STAGE 1957 – 1988	102
CHAPTER 20 THE RISE AND FALL OF THE LADIES 1946 – 1998	110

CHAPTER 21 TEAM MATCHES 1945 – 1998	119
CHAPTER 22 GRAPHITE SHAFTS, BIG BERTHA, AND THE MODERN GAME 1980 – 1998	126
CHAPTER 23 CLUB MATTERS 1970 – 1998	131
CONCLUSION THE MILLENNIUM AND BEYOND	139
APPENIDCES	142
LINDRICK ARTISANS CAPTAINS	143
CLUB OFFICIALS 1912 – 1998	144
MAJOR TROPHY WINNERS 1946 – 1998	145
OTHER TROPHY WINNERS 1977 – 1998	147
OTHER TROPHY WINNERS 1987 – 1998	149
ARTISAN TOURNAMENT (NORTHERN SECTION) 1945 – 1998	150
FIRST ANNUAL CIRCULAR ISSUED 1946	151
BIBLIOGRAPHY	153
INDEX	155

Part 1
1899 - 1945

CHAPTER 1
IN THE BEGINNING

The 19th Century was a period of great change in Britain, the Industrial Revolution, which had begun in the previous century, had, by the 1890's, transformed the nation in to the workshop of the world. With these industrial changes came great economic and social readjustment. Hours of work had become more regulated and people were starting to enjoy more leisure time as a result.

It was, therefore, in the late 19th century that sport became very popular as a means of exercise and relaxation. Football, Rugby, Tennis and Cricket all began to experience a period of rapid growth. The same was true of golf, but its history was much older.

Originating in Scotland, though there is some evidence dating back to 1530 to suggest it may have started in Holland, (according to historian Tom Scott), the game remained largely confined to Scotland until the 19th Century. Indeed, the first club in England was Royal Blackheath, which is believed to have been formed in 1766. Growth, however, remained very slow, because it was not until 1864 that the next club was formed in North Devon at Westward Ho!

This was a significant moment because in 1888 the first Artisan club was formed in North Devon and became known as Northam Artisan G. C. It was also important for two other reasons. Firstly, the club was founded by J. H. Taylor, winner of the Open Championship on five occasions and secondly, the fact that in 1921 he formed the Artisan Golfers Association.

By the 1890's golf was becoming widespread throughout the whole of England with about one hundred clubs known to be in existence. Thus, in 1891 golf came to Lindrick. The Sheffield and District Golf Club as it became known, was the first club in the Sheffield area and their choice of Lindrick as a site was inspired, because the land was natural golfing territory. The original course was laid out over nine holes and was being played by October 1891 but in the opposite direction to today, with the ninth green being on the site of the present Artisan clubhouse.

Over the next eight years the club started to become established with the local population, which was very important as the members were mainly from Sheffield and seen as outsiders. Nevertheless, relations grew with local landowners and other prominent people who were then admitted to the club. This was however only half the story, as it failed to take in to consideration the working population from the local villages and in particular those of Woodsetts, Shireoaks and Turnerwood.

When the club first opened the locals became involved almost straightaway, as they were able to earn a little extra income by caddying for the members, a tradition that still continues to this day. Photographic evidence owned by Miss Mary Milner and reproduced in J. Arthur-Colver's History of Lindrick Golf Club, shows local boys J. Allison, W. Colton, W. Betts and J. Cawkwell caddying for Sheffield and District members in the early 1890's. These were names that were soon going to feature in their own club; of course, little did they know it at the time!

On the back of fostering continued amity in the local community, point four of the Sheffield and District Golf Club's committee meeting held on May 9th, 1899, stated that, "it was proposed to form a working men's club at Woodsetts, [and] a resolution approving thereof was adopted".

It was a decision that was to be significant for the next one hundred years..

CHAPTER 2
A GAME OF THEIR OWN
1899 - 1912

Very little evidence exists of the golf played by the Artisans at the beginning of the century, indeed it is difficult to know what happened at all. One thing that is certain is that the club was not organised on anything like the lines of today and that the game was probably played on a casual basis without any formal competitions.

Nevertheless, it is clear that they did play with great enthusiasm and that some took it very seriously indeed. William Colton, who was mentioned in the previous chapter, had, by 1911 become so addicted that he had turned professional. This is known because his marriage certificate of that year states his profession as that of golfer. He was not on his own. James Brownlow, of Brancliffe Villas, Shireoaks, was also a professional golfer at a club in Staffordshire, but had started his golfing career as an employee at Lindrick and as an Artisan member.

Who exactly formed the club in 1899 is unclear, but it is believed that some of the players were those who had helped build the course. What is interesting is that many of these members resided outside the qualifying area, but at this time the regulations governing membership were only in the early stages of development and as a result there were no hard and fast rules on the matter for a number of years.

It is believed that the original membership was restricted to about a dozen or so men. Exactly who they were is uncertain, but it is probable that some of them may have been men such as, Sam Herrington, Jack Stothard, Tom Neal, Jarvis Allen, John Rowbottom, Bob Kay and George Bowles, who was the head greenkeeper at the time. The main occupations of these men varied, but some of them worked on the land or as gardeners for prominent local people. Jack Stothard, for example, was the gardener of the President George Denton. The other main occupation was the mining industry. The whole course was to become surrounded by collieries and many men worked at Shireoaks, Dinnington or Firbeck mines. The shiftwork patterns were an advantage, as either late starts or early finishes allowed them to play at the most convenient times.

At this time there were no clubhouse facilities and members only had two or three clubs at best, most of which they had made themselves. William Colton, for example, had won a competition between the best golfers from the Artisans with the prize being the job of Professional at Sandbeck golf course near Firbeck. This was the home of the Earl of Scarborough and William secured victory by defeating Arnold Taylor in the final. He was lucky. In his capacity of professional he had access to facilities no one else had and could therefore, make his own clubs. The other members simply had to make do with what they had and often they played with clubs made from ash sticks that were shaped to form a club and used balls that were made of wood. Unfortunately, there are no other records of matches played in this period, which lends itself to the conclusion that competitions were few and far between.

From a social point of view there were no clubhouse facilities during these early years and the Artisans, having played their round, simply carried their clubs home. As a result there was little or no inter-action, but members would relax in the Butchers Arms at Woodsetts or at the Station Hotel at Shireoaks. Naturally, the club remained rather fragmented.

William Colton driving from the first tee at Sandbeck, circa 1911.
Owned by Ellis Colton.

By 1912 it was clear that the club needed to be organised on a more formal basis with proper rules and competitions. It was the President, George Denton, took up the challenge of restructuring the club on more organised lines and the next chapter is about this process.

CHAPTER 3
THE CALM AND THE STORM
1912-1918

1912 was a significant year for the Artisans, as at last the fledgling club was began to spread its wings and become more organised.

The club's first general meeting of March 9th 1912 shows that there were twenty eight members, paying the princely sum of £3/7/ 6d in subscriptions, or 2/6d each. The President was George Denton, the Captain was Arnold Taylor, the Secretary was Jack Stothard and the Treasurer was Jarvis Allen. A committee also existed which comprised of R. Colton, Horace Cawkwell, James Brownlow and J. Shone. What exactly took place at this meeting is uncertain, but it would appear that it was a statement of membership and financial information. In 1913 the membership was the same, but one male member dropped out and was replaced by Miss A. Goacher, who thus became the club's first lady member. Revolutionary thinking indeed, after all, the Suffragette movement had only been established since 1903. Membership grew steadily and in 1914 it stood at 37, with £4 /12/ 6d being paid in subscriptions with Miss D. Goacher becoming the solitary lady member.

It would appear though that the club did have some basic structure prior to 1912, but it is very difficult to establish what this was. Rule cards, for example, were in existence, though sadly none of these have survived and were sold for a total of 4 shillings, but did actually cost 6/ 1 1/2 d to print! Golf clubs were also sold to the value of £3. From the golf point of view we know that team matches were being played, as refreshments for the Bulwell Artisans cost £1/ 7/ 6d and that the Secretary wrote to Welbeck Golf Club proposing a match, the stamp costing 1d! Overall, the profit on the year, which must be for 1911 was £1/ 5/ 2d, thus establishing the reputation of frugality of all subsequent Artisan Treasurers.

An interesting point passed at the 1913 meeting was that members must wear the club badge. It would appear that there was some difficulty, from the point of view of the Sheffield and District Golf Club, in determining who were and who were not Artisan members, and when they could play. This had been an issue for two or three years as the Secretary of the Sheffield and District Golf Club had written to the Artisans in March 1910 requesting the club not to play any matches in the week preceding or during the Yorkshire Union Championship.

The standard of golf being played was very different from that of today, but the level of competition was, nevertheless, just as fierce. Playing with clubs and balls that were hardly suitable for the job the matches played were often hard fought and involved, with several rounds being played before a winner was found. The Presidents Cup of 1912, for example, was started at the beginning of June and completed on Saturday 27th June, when Harry Goacher, 9 handicap, beat Horace Cawkwell, 1 handicap, in the final 3 & 1. This was significant because Horace Cawkwell was the best player in the club at the time, along with the young James Brownlow. The interest taken in the club by the President was very significant as George Denton himself presented the cup to Harry Goacher straight after the final. Interestingly though, it was not clear what the status of the cup was. The question was, did the winner get to keep the cup outright, or was it to be competed for on an annual basis?

The issue was resolved when Harry Goacher signed a sworn declaration stating that: " I agree to return the cup, presented by George Denton Esq., to Woodsetts Artisans Golf Club, to the Secretary of the above club, on or before the 30th day of December 1912."

Not that this mattered too much, because in April 1913 Harry won again beating Charlie Spencer 1 up after two halved matches. One could forgive him for being satisfied after that monumental effort, but this was not the case. In September 1913 the competition was played again and he was successful once more, this time beating Jack Stothard 2 & 1 after yet another halved match. As a fitting reward George Denton decided to present him with the cup outright.

Bearing in mind the level of wages at the time and also the lack of trophies being played for, many competitions were played for clubs and balls, as these were seen as worthy prizes, since they were expensive to buy. Indeed, these clubs were prized possessions and cherished dearly. James Brownlow, for example, in the Bogey competition of August 1912 won a club with a score of 83 net, playing off 3 handicap.

By early 1914 the tension in Europe was rising dangerously, as the threat of war came ever closer. The golf of the Artisans continued nevertheless. James Brownlow won the stroke competition in March with a score of 80 net, off 2 handicap, while the last two competitions won before the outbreak of war in August 1914 was a medal by Jack Stothard, winning a golf club given by Mr H. Crapper and William Colton, who won Mr A. E. Turnell's prize, finishing all-square in a bogey competition.

On August 4th 1914 Britain declared war on Germany. The world was never to be the same again and golf for the Artisans was not to re-start until the spring of 1919 after four years of the worst fighting conditions ever known.

CHAPTER 4
THE TWENTY'S 1919-1930

The First World War had exacted a great price on the nation. It had also exacted a great price on the Artisans. Many members had been called up for military service and many had paid the ultimate sacrifice.

James Brownlow, one of the best players in the club before the war, had joined the Royal Field Artillery and had been wounded firstly in the Easter uprising in Ireland in 1916, then killed with the rest of his gun crew on the 5th May, 1917 when his gun emplacement was hit by a shell. He was just 23.

Nevertheless, golf got back to normal and the first competitions started in April 1919 with a medal being played which was won by Arnold Taylor with a score of 87 net playing off 8 handicap. In total thirteen other players competed.

To make up for lost time the Artisans set about the Whitsun holiday in earnest. On Sunday June 8th a stroke competition was played and won by James Gowans, with a score of 81 gross, 78 net. It seemed ironic because Gowans was also the greenkeeper, proving once and for all that local knowledge was a distinct advantage and perhaps, during the war, while everyone else was thinking of other things, he had prepared hidden dangers that the other members had not been aware of! Proving that it was not a fluke he repeated his success in the bogey competition the following morning with a score of two down.

Also of interest was the result of the bogey foursomes when William Colton and Alec Betts lost to Robert Owen and Edward Knowles with a score of 7 down after having tied at 8 down. One can only assume that they played a further eighteen holes on the Sunday evening to determine the winners, as the first match had been played on Sunday afternoon! William Colton, you may recall, had been a professional at Sandbeck before the war, but this course had been taken up as agricultural land during the nations time of need. William, as a result of his misfortune, was forced to return to Lindrick and went to work in the coal industry, but this did not affect the quality of his golf, which remained very high.

By the summer of 1919 there were five scratch players in the club, these being William Colton, Arnold Taylor, Horace Cawkwell, Reg Ketley and James Gowans. The matches were now very well organised with prizes that were both practical and ornamental. Bob Jacobs, for example, who had become the professional at Lindrick in May 1919, (a name that was to become synonymous not just with golf at Lindrick, but also with the Artisans), presented three prizes, which comprised of a new club for first, two 2/6d balls for second and one ball for third! These were prized possessions as incomes were very poor at this time with the average wage being no more than £2 a week. No one went out and bought a new set of clubs and credit was very limited, so pieces of equipment, including balls, were gathered on a piece meal basis.

By the same token there were a few cups being played for. In 1919 a Lindrick member, R Edwin Eddison, who had joined Lindrick in May 1901 and who was a prominent Sheffield industrialist, presented a silver cup every year as a prize, second was a silver cigarette case, while third was a new club. The trophy was known as the Shireoaks Cup and the competition was a typical Artisan marathon played over three rounds in October under bogey. Played on Saturdays, the match was to start at 1p.m, raising the very interesting question of Artisan playing conditions, which at this point were not yet clear. One can only assume that this did not interfere with the play of the Sheffield and District Golf Club.

The first winner was Horace Cawkwell with an aggregate score of 11 down closely followed by Jack Stothard and Harry Kipling on 13 down. Over the years there were many other winners including Arnold and Frank Taylor, J. T. Rowbottom and Harry Goacher.

In about 1929, so the story goes, Eddison came upon hard times and his business folded with the result that he was ruined. In an attempt to regain his solvency he asked the Artisans to return the cups and found success in all but two cases.

Harry Goacher, who had won the cup in 1924, beating A. Hargreaves in the final which was played at Retford, and taking in to consideration the severity of the times, declined and kept the cup in his possession until his death in 1957. The Cup then remained in the

Past winners of the Shireoaks Cup, circa mid 1920's. Back to front; F. Taylor, J. T. Rowbottom, H. Goacher, E. Eddison and A. Taylor.
Owned by Lindrick Artisans Golf Club.

Goacher family until 1988 when his wife died. His daughter, Joyce, then came in to possession of the cup and decided to return it to the Artisans. Now the cup is played for annually and is presented to the leading Artisan on Captains Day in Harry Goachers memory. The second case was that of Henry Westby, who was the landlord at the Butchers Arms in Woodsetts. He had won the Shireoaks Cup in about 1923. Exactly why Eddison was unsuccessful is not known, maybe he gave a similar reply to Harry Goacher, or perhaps he simply lost track of who all the winners were. Either way the cup now belongs to his granddaughter, Miss Cynthia Herrington.

Harry Goacher, you may recall, had also won outright the Presidents Cup in 1914. This was replaced with a new trophy in 1924, which was known as the Presidents Bowl, and was won by non other than Harry Goacher who defeated S. White in the final! The Presidents Bowl, or the Rose Bowl as most members know it today, is now the oldest trophy that is still competed for by the Artisans and remains a 'major' in the Artisan golfing calendar.

The 1920's represented a time of hope after the Great War, but this was to be short lived. By 1926 unemployment was rising and the General Strike was pending. In the end the miners were left to themselves and this affected the Artisans as many members were employed in the coal industry.

Nevertheless, the golf continued and increasingly more prizes were available. Some were donated by the Vice-Presidents while some were given by the Artisans themselves. Sam Herrington, for example, the club Treasurer, gave a Guinea as first prize in a stroke competition in June 1924.

One of the most interesting aspects of the time was that if a trophy was given, there was often the stipulation that if a player was victorious on three occasion's then he was deemed to have won the cup outright. One of the most interesting stories of the period appertained to a trophy known as the Smith Cup.

This cup had been donated in 1914 by a Lindrick member, Gerard Kirke Smith, when it was first won by Reg Ketley who beat James Gowans in the final. Due to the war it was not played again until 1919 when Frank Taylor beat William Colton by 1up. The competition always attracted a large entry and inevitably the best players in the club reached the final. In fact, it was so important that the final warranted two referees for it. The 1920 final was a classic, as Frank Taylor beat Joe Twibell by 1 hole after a tie. With a hatrick awaiting, Frank lost in the first round of 1921 to H. Betts by 5 & 4. He was fated never to win it again.

By 1924 a new group of players had started to make their mark in the club. The 1923 match was won by William Merrick who beat Ted Highfield in the final by 4 & 2, but the man to beat in the mid 1920's was Cliff Herrington. The son of Sam Herrington, Cliff won the cup in 1924 beating Fred Finbow in the final. Not content with this he repeated the feat in 1927, winning not only the cup, but also the first prize of twenty-five shillings and followed it up with his third victory in 1929 beating Lloyd Merrick by 3 & 2. The cup is now the proud possession of his son, Ken Herrington, who was also a member of the Artisans in the '60's and '70's.

In January 1928 the President, George Denton died. It was a tremendous shock, not just for the Artisans but also the Sheffield and District Golf Club, where he had been Secretary, Captain and Vice-President during his time. As a mark of respect the Artisans donated five shillings towards the funeral expenses. However, the golf continued, just as George Denton would have wanted. The new President was another leading figure from the parent club, Douglas Leng, who in October 1928, agreed to donate a cup for annual competition. This trophy, known simply as the Leng Cup, remains, along with the Presidents Bowl, as the two oldest trophy's still competed for by the Artisans today. The value of this trophy should not be underestimated as it was played over four rounds of medal on one weekend, thirty six holes per day from the back tees. The cup itself was valued in 1929 at £30, an extraordinary amount of money for the time.

Meanwhile, other matches continued to be played. On Wednesday, 28th April 1926 the Artisans played in the Sheffield Team Championship, when Frank Taylor, Ted Highfield, Cliff Herrington and William Merrick represented the club. The Committee also agreed that "a little remuneration would be given" due to lost time. Unfortunately, they declined to say how much this was! The result of the match also remains unknown.

Other local tournaments were attended on an individual basis, with varying degrees of success. Perhaps the most famous of these was the Banning Cup, which is still played at the Tinsley Park Golf Club in Sheffield to this day. The course had only been open since 1920 and was quite novel in the sense that it was a municipal course and one of the first such in England. In 1922 Arnold Cawkwell won the competition.

Another area where the club was competing was at the Northern Artisan Tournament. By 1927 the National Association had been in existence some six years, but it was felt that a northern section was required due to the travelling distances required to compete in matches that were based largely around the Home Counties. With the emphasis on the best players representing the club a qualifying competition was played over strokes for entry in to either the first or second class sections based upon handicap. In some instances two qualifying rounds were played, as in 1928, when the tournament was held at Prestbury, in Cheshire. Additionally, £5 was given as expenses!

Thus, by 1929 the structure of the playing side of the club was well established with many prizes being competed for and the major trophy's being the Presidents Bowl, the Leng Cup, the Shireoaks Cup and the soon to be lost Smith Cup. With this strong base in place the club could look forward to the 1930's with confidence that their playing prowess was healthy. The same could not, however, be said about the world economy. Nevertheless, the Artisans golfed on.

Club trophies circa 1929.
From left to right. Shireoaks Cup 1924 won by Harry Goacher, now presented to the leading Artisan on Captains Day, Lennox Dixon Cup 1934 won by Leonard Kipling, Smith Cup 1929 won by Cliff Herrington, Lennox Dixon Cup 1937 won by Reginald Colton and the Shireoaks Cup 1923 won by Henry Westby. In 1929 the Smith Cup had been won outright and the Shireoaks Cup had been discontinued. This was replaced by the Dixon Cup.
Owned by the author.

CHAPTER 5
TEAM MATCHES 1912-39

During the first ten years of the club few team matches were played and it was not until the first annual general meeting in 1912 that there is any mention of playing matches against other clubs.

The financial statement shows that £1/7/6d was spent on refreshments for the Nottingham based Bulwell Artisans team, but does not record the result. We must presume that this was for the 1911 season. However, in July 1912 the Artisans played Bulwell again: and lost, 6 1/2 to 3 1/2! Notable losers were Horace Cawkwell, Reg Ketley and Jack Stothard, but winners included the youthful James Brownlow and the fifteen year old Harry Goacher. At this time it seemed Bulwell was the only match being played away from home because in July 1914, just one month before the outbreak of the First World War, the Artisans played in Nottingham. Arriving probably by train, with their clubs on their backs, they were promptly defeated 6 1/2 to 3 1/2. Stung by this, a return was organised and played on August 15th, eleven days after the outbreak of war. The result was an Artisan win by 7 matches to 2, it was a poignant moment, as it was the last competitive match played until the Spring of 1919.

The first known match against The Sheffield and District Golf Club was played in May 1914 when the Artisans lost by 11 matches to 5, but it was not until April 1921 that the Sheffield and District Golf Club instructed the Match Secretary to:

"Arrange two matches with Woodsetts Artisans, one to be held in May and one in September".

That first game of 1914 was a very serious affair, with ten singles played in the morning and five foursomes in the afternoon. Only Reg Ketley and James Brownlow were able to win their singles, while in the foursomes just Horace Cawkwell and William Colton, as well as Arnold Taylor and Jack Rich, triumphed. The Sheffield and District team comprised of some interesting personnel, such as Douglas Leng, who was to be a future president, Harold Eardley, who was one of Lindrick's best ever players and G. K. Smith, who lived at Wigthorpe House at Carlton-in-Lindrick, and who was another Artisan benefactor.

The match of October 1919 was very interesting too. The match was lost 17 to 14 with the afternoon foursomes proving decisive. Winners on the Artisan side were Reg Ketley, James Gowans; (who claimed the scalp of Harold Eardley), Arnold and Frank Taylor as well as Arthur Robinson and Tom Neal. On the Artisan team that day were the professionals Bob Jacobs and the former Hallamshire professional George Cawkwell, a relation of Arnold and Horace. Not that it made much difference, as Bob Jacobs lost 3 & 2 and George Cawkwell lost 2 & 1 while in the foursomes, as playing partners, they lost by one hole to the combination of Bernard Wragg and Douglas Leng.

The Worksop Guardian describes how after the match the Artisans were entertained to dinner in the Sheffield and District clubhouse, a tradition that continues in the twice annual match to this day. George Denton was in the Chair and addressed the teams, describing how there was a good feeling between the clubs and how pleased he was to hear that the Artisans now had fifty seven members and were in a financially good position. As was typical of the time an impromptu entertainment followed consisting of songs, recitations and dancing. The musical accompaniment was by J. H. Coldwell.

The Artisan team that played against the Sheffield and District Golf Club in 1919.

Owned by Lindrick Artisans Golf Club

During the 1930's the Artisans became a force to be reckoned with, particularly in matches played against the Sheffield and District Golf Club. In the years between 1930 and 1938, there was only one year, 1937, when the Artisans lost. Of interest also is the fact that although there was the stipulation of 1921 that the match should be played twice a year there were three occasion's during the 1930's when only one game was played. If there was a reason for this, then it is, unfortunately, unknown.

Although the Artisans dominated these years it would be a mistake to assume that the matches were one sided. The match of 1931 was very close indeed. The first match was played on 28th March, with the Artisans trailing 11 games to 12. Ted Highfield had managed to beat Sheffield and District Captain Tom Sorby, but by the same token F. A. Neil had defeated R. O. Spencer. The return, played on October 24th was a titanic struggle resulting in an Artisan victory by 12 1/2 to 9 1/2, making the overall result 23 1/2 to 21 1/2 to the Artisans.

The 1932 match was a big Artisan win, but more notable by the fact that in the second game, which was played in July, a new member took to the field, a certain R. Rowett, a man who was to play in the match for the next fifty years, give or take a year or two. Nevertheless, it was an inauspicious start as he lost 2 and 1 to F. H. Wilkinson. Also at this time the match was played off level, so the "draw" was organised to match players of equal ability. Again, this tradition was to continue up until the 1980's, before it was changed and matches are now played under handicap.

By the early 1920's other team matches had become well established and competitions were being played not just against Sheffield and District and Bulwell, but also Retford, Tinsley Park (the new municipal club in Sheffield), Brown Bayleys (the steel firm in Sheffield), Welbeck, Beauchief (also in Sheffield) and Worksop Golf Club.

Against Retford in 1919, for example, playing home and away, the aggregate result was 17 matches to 5, while against Worksop the result was 8 matches to 7. Interestingly, one of the players on the Retford team that day was Edwin Eddison, the same man who had donated the Shireoaks Cups to the club and who in a few years time was to ask for them back when his business folded.

Some interesting matches were played against Brown Bayleys and

Welbeck in the 1930's. On the 13th June 1930 (at Lindrick) the Artisans won by 10 matches to 6, with notable victories from Tommy Widdison, Jim Waterhouse, Alf Randall, Jack Inman and Vic Parkinson. However, it was not always that way. In the match of May 1931 the Artisans played at Handsworth in Sheffield and lost in a close match by 8 matches to 6. Meanwhile, in August 1930 the Artisans played Welbeck who were decisively beaten by 12 matches to 1. Welbeck's solitary winner on that day was H. Atkinson who beat Ernest Mappin. Of note also was the quality of the course, which was described as being in "excellent condition" as well as the fact that the match was played in a competitive manner, but was both "interesting and enjoyable", according to the Worksop Guardian report.

Games played against Beauchief tendered to have similar outcomes. There were large Artisan victories in 1931 and 1932 when the Artisans won by 13 matches to 3 and 13 matches to 2. Occasionally Beauchief would be successful, as in the match of June 1931 which was played on the old Abbeydale course at Sheffield when the Artisans lost easily by 10 matches to 5.

Tougher competition was to be had from Worksop Golf Club, who played the Artisans on many occasions during the 1930's. At the end of August 1930, for example, the Artisans lost a close match at Worksop by $5\frac{1}{2}$ to $3\frac{1}{2}$, but won in the return match at Lindrick, which was played on September 3rd by $5\frac{1}{2}$ to $4\frac{1}{2}$.

The same was also true of matches played against the Artisans from the Pennine club of Buxton and High Peak. The match of 31st May, 1931 resulted in a heavy loss for the Woodsetts Artisans by 11 matches to 4. The game was an all day affair, comprising of both foursomes and singles. A very serious match indeed!

Clearly these matches promoted great competitive rivalry. No one wanted to lose, but the games were also played in the best of spirits, which had the benefit of developing new friendships that would last for many years.

CHAPTER 6
CLUB BUSINESS 1924-1939

There is no documentary evidence of club business between 1899 and 1912 and that which does exist after 1912 gives little details other than odd rules or agreements. What can be said with certainty is that there were committee meetings and that these were held on a regular basis.

This is known because the financial statement of 1913 shows that 7s 6d was paid to Mrs Stothard, who was the wife of the Secretary and Treasurer Jack Stothard, and that the meetings were held in Birkett Wood Cottage which was their home. Unfortunately, there are no records of these meetings, but it is known that the Head Greenkeeper, James Gowans, showed them the basic principals of bookkeeping for the purposes of the accounts.

By 1924 the club was functioning on more organised lines and meetings were documented and records kept. By this time there were approximately ten members of the committee who were kept busy with the general running of the club. Some of this was the scheduling of the competitions, while other matters were concerned with the functioning of the club. For example, on the 16th March, 1924 the committee, on the proposition of William Merrick and seconded by Horace Cawkwell, agreed that:

"Private members have [the] power to bring grievances to committee. If not rectified [they have the] power to ask for a general meeting to be called if twelve or more are in favour of [the] same."

It was a far reaching rule; a rule that has remained ever since and has, on numerous occasions, been required to help solve major issues. Put simply, it made the elected committee accountable at any time, other than just at the annual general meeting when offices were being elected.

Meanwhile, the lack of clarity on playing conditions was resolved in 1922 when the Sheffield and District Golf Club stipulated that no Artisan must play with a non-member without the permission of the Lindrick club. The Parent Club then wrote to the Artisans to ask for a full list of members and their addresses because, in their opinion, the:

"numbers authorised had been exceeded and no further members were to be elected until a decision had been reached by the committee".

The Artisan committee quickly realised that the issue needed to be tackled immediately and on the 30th May agreed that the secretary should meet the Sheffield and District club about "making rules for the use of the Artisans [and] each member to receive a copy". To make the point an offending member was fined one shilling for playing with a non-member, a timely reminder that privileges should not be exceeded. To assist in ensuring that the rules were observed new club badges were bought from a company called Fatorini and Sons of Bradford, but each member had to purchase their own at the price of 1s 6d each.

Thus, the Sheffield and District Committee meeting of May 1922 established the following rules:

- "No new members to be elected to the Woodsetts Artisans Golf Club until the number of members are reduced to eighty, including women and juveniles. Juveniles must be 15 years of age or over"
- "No matches to be fixed for Saturdays or Sundays. If exception is made by the Committee in any case the match to be limited to 12 a side."
- "Ladies and juveniles not to play on Saturdays and Sundays"
- "All members to wear the club badge adopted by the committee of the Woodsetts Artisans Golf Club when playing."
- "All members to assist in protecting the course and report anyone playing who is not a member."

These rules were a significant change because the haphazard system of ad hoc gentleman's agreements were simply unworkable. Not that this solved everything. The 1899 resolution establishing a workingmen's club at Woodsetts had by precedence come to involve both Shireoaks and Turnerwood. This felt natural as all three villages surrounded the course. However, in 1930 applications were received from four men who lived at Dinnington. It was an interesting point. Many Woodsetts men worked at Dinnington Colliery, Harry Goacher, for example, was an electrician there and it is easy to conclude that friendships were made and Dinnington men became interested in playing golf at a place and a price they could afford. The Sheffield and

District Club discussed this at their committee meeting of March 1930 and rejected the applications and stated very clearly that:
"Artisan membership is confined only to Woodsetts, Turnerwood and Shireoaks."

Ordinarily this would have been the end of the issue, but it rumbled on for the next eighteen months, when at the Sheffield and District Committee meeting of September 1931 Tom Sorby raised the matter again on behalf of the Artisans. Once again it was agreed that the Dinnington four could not join. It seemed ironic because in 1938 Sir Albert Bingham, a very distinguished Artisan benefactor, requested that three of his employees be accepted in to the club who did not meet the entry qualifications. It was a very difficult decision, since Bingham had just donated to the club the Challenge Cup and as a consequence the committee, "under the circumstances.....had no alternative but to accept them." Thus, John and Percy Pick as well as C. T. Tant became members, though interestingly they never actually played.

1930 was a watershed year in other ways too. The Annual General Meeting held on the 13th December took place in the Chauffeurs room, a small part of the Lindrick clubhouse. This was because the Artisan clubhouse was in very poor condition. The meeting was significant for a number of other reasons. Firstly, those members who were running the club were of the "old school", people such as Sam Herrington and Tom Neal. But a new generation had come in to the club in the 1920's, men such as Leonard Kipling, Joe Mee, George Herrington and Jack Clarkson. It was time for the baton to be passed on. Secondly, because the meeting itself was shrouded in confusion between when it should be held and by the fact that both the Secretary and Treasurer were absent through illness.

Originally planned for the 20th, it had been switched at very short notice to the 13th by the Chairman, R. O. Spencer. Some members felt that this was unsatisfactory. To make matters worse Vic Parkinson and Tommy Widdison arrived at 7 P.M., but the meeting had actually been scheduled to start at 6.30 P.M., when only ten members were present. It was a charged atmosphere in the small confines of the Chauffeurs room, but after a lengthy discussion it was agreed that the meeting should proceed. It was in these circumstances that Leonard

Kipling proposed and Joe Mee seconded that due to Tom Neal's illness that Jack Clarkson should become Secretary. Jack was reluctant at first, believing it was unfair to take another mans job without him being able to defend himself, but was persuaded in the end to accept the post. Apart from a short period between 1932 and 1933 Jack was to hold the post until his retirement in 1978.

At the same time costs had remained fairly static over the years and the club subscription had stayed at the conservative sum of 2s 6d since 1912. 1928 was, therefore, a bit of a shock as the A.G.M held on the 17th December 1927 proposed the raising of the subscription to 5s! The club minutes give no reason why, and there was no debate. It must have been carried however, as the subscription for both 1929 and 1930 was also 5s. Still, after the initial shock the subscription was to rise by only 2d over the next ten years.

Other issues requiring financial support was charity. In 1926 10s was sent to the hospital fund, while in 1927 this was raised to 10/6d. In the following years a charity competition was organised with the proceeds being split with two thirds going to Sheffield and the remainder going to Worksop. It was an important point because at this time there was no National Health Service and care was funded through private insurance. This strong sense of caring extended to the members also, indeed each member was insured at 4d whilst playing at Lindrick and 5d for away matches.

Additionally, money was paid to those members who had been injured whilst at work.. The A. G. M of 1936 agreed to pay £2/10s to both Leonard Kipling and Sam Herrington who were ill. It was further agreed that:

"If any other member should be off work any considerable time, either by accident or illness, a grant should be made and a special general meeting should be called to decide such grant".

In May 1937 both George Kipling and George Spencer received a grant due to injury and it was agreed that the qualifying period be sixteen weeks. However, the 1937 A. G. M decided to discontinue the grant and agreed instead to replace it with a charity competition to be played as and when required. This had the advantage of raising more money and did away with the need to call a special general meeting.

The membership issue of 1922, had, by 1932 been resolved. Natural wastage had reduced the membership from ninety six to a new total of eighty. This was made up of sixty men and twenty women. In addition a process was started whereby long serving members were given honorary status. The first known honorary member was Sam Herrington in 1931 as was the Professional, Jack Jacobs, in 1937. Jack wrote to the club saying that "he appreciated it very much". It was to be 1946 before the former Secretary, Tom Neal was to receive the same honour.

Nevertheless, by 1932 the club was feeling more confident and on the proposition of George Herrington and seconded by Leonard Kipling it was agreed to approach the Sheffield and District Golf Club about the possibility of increasing the membership. The request was put formally in writing and was discussed at the Sheffield and District committee meeting of 1st February 1932, when it was agreed to leave the matter in the hands of Harold Eardley, Basil Gray and the Secretary, Major Sutton. H. Lowe. In March 1932 the Sheffield and District Golf Club agreed that:

"the number of new Artisan members be increased by 10. It was especially mentioned at the meeting that the badges must be worn by all members".

This increased the total membership to ninety, a figure it was to remain at for the next forty seven years. In the event only nine new members were elected, but notable names joining the ranks were Roy Rowett, the Spencer brothers William and Alan, along with the Herrington's, Stuart and Harry.

Although the club was running reasonably smoothly, there was the feeling that the business of the club was being left to just a few people and that there was distinct feeling of apathy amongst some of the members. The A. G. M of 1932 was held in Woodsetts School in the hope that there would be a better attendance and as the minutes from that meeting suggest:

"This action did induce more members to attend, but there is still not enough interest taken by the majority of the members in the interests of the club."

The depth of feeling on this issue continued and in 1934 the A. G. M passed a rule that if a member did not send a written apology for not attending the meeting he would be fined 1s which would be added to the annual subscription!

However, relations with the Sheffield and District Golf Club, which were a little unsteady in 1922 were now very good. Many fires had been started on Lindrick in 1934 and the Artisans were asked to keep a look out for the fire raisers. A notice to the same effect was also put in the Worksop Guardian, while in 1936 persistent ball stealing at the 13th and 14th holes required two members to patrol these holes between 2 P.M. and 5 P.M. every Sunday. Thus, the reputation of the club as the course policeman was born. The strength of the two clubs pulling together was shown in late 1939, two months after the outbreak of W.W.II, when the Artisans agreed to help the Parent Club in running the course due to reduced staff. The Artisan committee felt that this would " cement the good relationship that existed between the Artisans and the Sheffield and District Golf Club".

Tom Sorby had taken over as President from Douglas Leng, who had died in 1933 and the club steered a steady course through the 1930's as Hitler's armies began their remorseless conquest of the European continent. Very soon the Artisans were to have some tough years in front of them. Years that they would handle with honour, pride and dignity.

CHAPTER 7
GOLF IN THE 30'S 1930-1939

In October 1929 the New York Stock Exchange crashed, but as the economy and industry declined, the Artisans flourished. In fact, in many ways, these were vintage years as the quality of the golf simply became better and better. Indeed, it is fair to say that during this peroid the club came of golfing age.

R. Eddison, who had donated to the club a new Shireoaks Cup every year since the early 1920's, had fallen on hard times and withdrew his patronage and reclaimed several of the trophy's from the members. At the A. G. M of 1930 it was proposed that a new club knockout trophy be played for and that it be bought from Mr Lennox Dixon, who was a Vice President at the time.

For the next nine years this cup was played and there were several notable winners, including Leonard Kipling, Reg Colton, William Randall and Horace Merrick, who was a winner on two occasions. Also of note was the performance of Norman Tyson, who won the trophy in his first full season in the club in 1938.

Due to the general lack of cup's and trophy's being played for, the Artisans also decided to have a cup of their own. The firm of Walker and Hall were approached as, in the words of the committee, they "would knock 50% off the price". The budget was set at £12 and their representative, Mr Cutts, was requested to "get the best terms possible". In the event the final cost was £11 which included both plinth and engraving. This represented extremely good value for money to the frugal Artisans.

Leonard Kipling winner of the Lennox Dixon Cup 1934.
Owned by Roy Kipling.

It was proposed by Vic Parkinson and seconded by George Herrington that if a member should win the Artisans cup three times, not necessarily consecutively, then he should be allowed to keep it. It was an interesting point, because in the past this had not always been specified until after the event, but had, to some degree, become an accepted practice. However, in hindsight this was not a very good idea, as by 1934 it had been won outright by Charlie Colton! It thus became the shortest lived trophy that as ever been played for by the Artisans.

This was not to be the only example of this problem. In 1928 George Denton had died and the position of President was filled by Douglas Leng who donated his own trophy to the club. As usual the practice of a player winning the cup three times was in place, but in 1933 Leng died suddenly, and as a mark of respect the A. G. M of 1933 stated that:

" The cup of the late Mr D. C. Leng remain in the club as a memento of our late President, and that it never be won outright."

This was unfortunate, because Horace Merrick had won the trophy twice up this point (1930 and 1932), and then again in 1937, when he won it for a third time. It seemed only fitting however, to mark this achievement with some form of recognition. Thus, it was decided to present Horace with a silver replica which his widow still proudly owns to this day.

The 1932 win was notable by the fact that after fifty four holes he was eleven shots off the lead, which was held by Arnold Cawkwell on 224. Horace's winning score was 311 beating Lloyd Merrick in to second place on 312, with Arnold Cawkwell a shot further back.

The 1931 competition was also very interesting. Twenty four players started the competition in the first round, but after seventy two holes only eight players had completed their cards. The cup was won by Ernest Mappin, whose four round score was 300, which comprised rounds of 79, 76, 70, and 75. His winning score was also eighteen shots better than Horace Merrick's winning score the previous year. Second that year behind Ernest Mappin was Jim Merrick jnr, Horace's brother, who in his first season in the club shot a six at the last hole to lose by one shot!

Apart from team matches the Artisans were also involved in

playing local tournaments against players from other clubs. Perhaps the most prestigious of these was the Sheffield Telegraph Cup. This competition was run by The Sheffield Telegraph newspaper, which at this time was owned the Artisan President D.C. Leng, and was open to players from clubs that lay in a twenty five mile radius of Sheffield. Before the Second World War the competition was divided in to two sections for low and high handicap players. Those in the high category competed for the Telegraph Trophy, while those in the low category played for the Telegraph Cup.

In July 1931 the tournament was held at Lindrick and after thirty six holes of medal play Harry Goacher finished a close second in the low handicap category. He was followed closely by several other Artisan golfers that day, including Harry Pollard, Arnold Cawkwell, Frank Colton and Horace Merrick. Three years later it was the turn of the high handicap players to shine. This time Jack Neal, who was the son of Tom Neal, finished an unlucky second to C. Kaye from Lees Hall. Played at the Rotherham Golf Club at Thrybergh, both players tied with a score of 141 but Kaye was deemed the winner by virtue of the fact that he had a superior first round score.

Another near miss was to occur in July 1937 when Charlie Colton was to finish second to A. Richard Westerman, whose score of 147 was good enough to win by one stroke. Played at Lindrick once more, several Artisans competed, and in particular the Colton family. The Worksop Guardian report described how:

"William Colton, his son Reginald, and nephews Charles and Frank Colton, formed an interesting quartet. Members of Woodsetts Artisans Club, they [were] all ex-caddies."

The report continued by saying:

" Charles Colton, handicapped at three, made a great bid with a second round gross score of 75, while his uncle was well in the running until he encountered trouble at the 15th. Reginald had pretty much the same experience."

The sense of disappointment was immense, but all of this was invaluable experience and the clubs "nearly man" image was to be avenged after the war, when ironically, Ellis Colton, another son of William, was to triumph in the Telegraph Cup and Norman Tyson was to win the Telegraph Trophy.

At the same time the Artisans also competed in other competitions. Another success was that of Audley Clarkson who won the Marchioness of Titchfield Cup in 1939 at Welbeck. In the modern age, when bandits abound, spare a thought for a an old master whose net score of 64, playing off 18 handicap, was good enough to secure first place from Dr P. J. Quigley of Bessecar, whose score of 68 net, playing off 16 handicap, was simply not good enough!

In 1936 the Artisans received a new trophy to play for when Mrs Kayser, who was an Artisan Vice President, donated the Kayser Cup for annual competition. This cup, which is still competed for today, is the third "major" of the club and has a most interesting history. At the annual tea and prize presentation of November 1935 Mrs Kayser was invited to present the prizes and trophies to that years winners. The words of the Worksop Guardian report sum up neatly the mood of the moment and explain how the Kayser Cup came in to being when it said:

"Mrs Kayser said it gave her great pleasure to present the prizes, and after doing so she promised to give another cup to replace the Artisans Cup recently won outright. Her kind offer was received with loud applause!"

In many ways the new competition was the ultimate challenge as on the one hand it was designed to test a players stroke play, while on the other it also tested his matchplay prowess. Thus, the first two rounds were played as medal, with the top eight qualifying for the matchplay stages. Here though was the interesting part: after the quarter and semi finals had been played at Lindrick the final was then competed for at Retford Golf Club! This was because the Kayser family lived at Eaton Hall just outside Retford, and as well as being members of Lindrick they were also members at Retford! The winner would therefore, be the ultimate champion. It was also stipulated that if a player was to win it three times consecutively then it would become his own property. At the end of the competition those attending should, in the words of the committee:

"Proceed to Eaton Hall where they will be the guests of Mrs Kayser."

The Kayser Cup was first played for then in 1936 when the winner was William Randall. Who he beat in the final remains a mystery as there are no records of this match. Nevertheless, over the next three years he was joined by Harry Pollard, Cliff Herrington and Ernest Mappin as the competitions pre war winners.

Just a year before the outbreak of W.W.II the Artisans received two further trophy's to play for. These were the Challenge Cup, which was donated by Sir Albert Bingham and the Commonside Foursomes which were given by Harold Eardley and Geoffrey Gullick. It is not known who the pre war winners of the foursomes were, but the Challenge Cup was won first won by Reg Colton in 1938, George Merrick in 1939 and Frank Stothard in 1940. Still competed for today, these trophy's have become the fourth and fifth "majors" respectively.

Meanwhile, it was during this time that the Artisan Golfers Association (Northern Section) came in to being and the Artisans started to compete. Little is known of their exploits, but in June 1938 six members competed at Hillside at Southport, an area of the country that still remains a centre of Artisan golf today. Walter Neal, son of Tom Neal, scored 148 as did Oscar Clarkson. Oscar was also on the Northern Section executive committee at this time, but it was to be his brother Jack, who was to become the most influential person in the Northern Association in the immediate post war years.

By 1939 the international situation had declined and general European war, which had threatened for much of the 1930's, was soon to become a reality. The Artisans were to play their role in this, but in the high summer of 1939 it was possible to say that the club was now well established, with numerous trophies and prizes to play for, a reputation for playing hard in team matches, but always fair and courteous to its opponents, and above all, confident that a bright future lay ahead of it. The Second World War was to ask many questions of the Artisans, but never once did they waiver from their duty confident in their belief that as soon as the war was over they could return to their favourite pastime.

CHAPTER 8
CLUBHOUSE DEVELOPMENTS 1919-1939

There were no clubhouse facilities in 1899, indeed it was not until 1919 that even the basic facilities existed. Between these times members simply carried the few clubs they owned under their arms and cycled home after they had finished their round.

Thus, on July 14th 1919 the Secretary of the Sheffield and District Golf Club read a letter from the:

"Honorary Secretary of the Artisans Golf Club asking for permission to occupy land near the first tee by erecting a small club room. Mr Denton proposed, Mr Eardley seconded that the Captain and Honorary Secretary interview J. Gowans (Honorary Secretary of the Artisans G. C.) and arrange for accommodation."

This meeting took place, though there is no record of what was said, but on the 26th July 1919 the Parent club agreed that:

"It was resolved to grant the Artisans Golf Club two bays of the motor shed at the end (furthest from the clubhouse) for premises."

According to an Artisan Golfer article written by Jack Clarkson and Roy Kipling in 1968, it is understood that the new premises were made of wood and the total cost of conversion was £54. Half of this was put up by the Parent Club and £10 was lent by Arthur Hargreaves who was the father of Bob Jacobs wife, Vivian. The loan was repaid by raising money through whist drives and dances.

By comparison to today the accommodation was very basic. Essentially the structure was about twenty four feet by sixteen feet. One side was open to allow access by motor cars and there was an earthen floor. It was not until 1923 that any furniture was added and this consisted of just a few chairs and a large table. No bar facilities existed but some "bootleg" beer was sold in bottles as time moved on. Nevertheless, the Artisans now had the rudiments of their own clubhouse and this started the process of improvements that have continued to this day.

With this rise in status came increased responsibility. The building had to be insured against fire, and this was duly done in 1926 by

William Merrick; who, at a cost of 21 Shillings, took out a policy with the Royal Insurance Co. Ltd. By 1939 costs had driven this up to £1 15s 3d. Still, it did give peace of mind!

Progress was, however, quite slow. It was difficult to hold meetings in the clubroom as it did not really have the facilities required and often meetings were held elsewhere. The 1930 A. G. M, for example, was held in the chauffeurs room at the back of the Sheffield and District Golf Club due to the poor state of the Artisan clubhouse.

This came to a head in 1932 when a special meeting was called to discuss the conditions of sanitation. In a precedent that ran against normal club practice, the ladies committee was asked to be present. This was a good idea and quite far reaching for the times, as it was the ladies who had raised the issue due to the problem of entertaining their opponents. Strongly supported by Arnold Cawkwell, who was on the committee, it was agreed that the club should have a toilet so long as the ladies agreed to pay £5 towards the alterations. A plan was drawn up supervised by Vic Parkinson, Harry Goacher and Jack Clarkson. A letter was drafted to the Parent Club by Jack Clarkson, which was discussed at the Sheffield and District committee meeting of 1st February 1932, where the matter was referred to the House committee for further discussion. In March 1932 permission was granted and the work was completed by the firm of Middletons at cost of £21/15s! A. E Turnell of the Parent Club had over seen the project and the Artisan committee acknowledged his assistance with a letter of thanks. As a result of the cost of installing the toilet a fund was established in 1934 to help pay for clubhouse improvements and a caretaker appointed to be paid the annual sum of 15s, with the ladies section contributing 5s!

The next major project was the installation of the electric light. There were a number of reasons for this. Firstly, many of the existing oil lamps needed replacing while secondly, there was always the risk of fire. The electric light, which was still seen as a relatively new convenience had the advantage of being relatively cheap, represented the future and was safe. Thus, at the committee meeting of September 25th 1937, on the proposition of Arnold Cawkwell, seconded by Oscar Clarkson, the decision to install an electric light was accepted. Harry Goacher, who was an electrician at Dinnington colliery, agreed to take up the project, while the ladies section was asked to contribute part of the cost. On October 1st the installation was completed for the royal sum of £2/8/9d, of which the ladies contributed 10s. At the committee meeting held on the 16th October Arnold Cawkwell:

"Expressed his appreciation and thanks to the Secretary and Chairman for the prompt way they had dealt with the installation of the electric light".

Modifications were to continue and the following year Harry Goacher installed an electric stove to accompany the new light. Furniture was improved with the purchase of two dozen chairs from a company called D. G. Tischell and Sons Ltd for the club room in 1936. However, controversy came to surround these chairs as thirteen were found to be defective. The issue rumbled on for some while and by October, having had the company's representative to inspect the chairs, the committee was forced to state that:

"If a favourable reply was not forthcoming within seven days further proceedings would be taken."

The club minutes make no more reference to this issue, so it is fair to conclude that a favourable resolution was found as there is no record of any litigation being filed against Tischell's for supplying unsatisfactory goods!

With clubhouse developments moving slowly on it was now possible to use the facilities, not only to relax in after playing golf, but also for social occasions as well. In August 1931 for example, the Artisans played a match against Buxton at Lindrick and the club room was used to prepare and serve the meals. It is interesting for two reasons. Firstly, the match was played on a Sunday, starting at 12 Noon, followed by lunch with play resuming at 3 P. M. and tea at 7 P. M.! Secondly, it was important because the club needed to "borrow a few tables, chairs and crockery from the church institute". Also of interest was the fact that the meals were provided by Mrs Mappin, who was the wife of the greenkeeper, Tommy Mappin, who had replaced James Gowans in 1921.

Up until this point social events did not really exist, but with improved clubhouse facilities it was decided to hold a prize presentation and social evening in October 1933. Held in the Artisan clubhouse the President, Tom Sorby, was in attendance, and the meal was provided by Vic Parkinson who was assisted by six lady helpers. Whether or not they were lady members is not known, but it is very likely they were and to this day many of the lady members assist on Captains Day and Invitation Day. Also of interest was the fact that nine gallons of beer had been ordered along with two dozen bottled beers and three dozen mineral waters.

This evening must have been reasonably successful, as at the Annual General Meeting which followed, it was proposed by Leonard Kipling and seconded by George Herrington that an annual social and prize presentation be held each year.

In following years entertainers were employed, for example in 1935, the Sharpe Brothers were employed and a pianist as well as a piano accordionist was sought. The loan of a piano was organised through Ernest Mappin, while in 1936 the comedian Billy Wade was commissioned at a cost of 11s and the tenor R. Deizall was paid 7/6d for entertaining the club.

The piano of Ernest Mappin, who was the son of Tommy Mappin, remained in the club room for many years and very often entertainment would be instigated at a moments notice. The prime mover in this was a young man called Horace Merrick. Apart from being an excellent golfer he was also a fine pianist, though not schooled in the art by training, Horace had a natural ear for music and was able to play just about any piece without too much difficulty. His love of the piano and music in general was not just confined to the Artisans. At the Butchers Arms public house in Woodsetts he would often be asked to entertain the people. Though sometimes this was inconvenient, he never refused, as he genuinely enjoyed it so much. More to the point, his listeners appreciated it too. This tradition continued for the next forty years until Horace's untimely death in 1975.

By 1939, at the outbreak of W.W.II, the Artisans had a clubhouse that was reasonably comfortable with most of the conveniences of the day to hand. It was now possible to relax after a game without having to walk home first and it was also possible to entertain visiting teams in some semblance of comfort that was acceptable to all. W.W.II was to distract the Artisans from the maintenance of the clubhouse for the next six years and the story of the clubhouses' development after the war will be told in another chapter.

CHAPTER 9
LADY ARTISAN GOLFERS 1913-39

The history of the Artisans can not be told without some reference to the lady members of the club. Although they have their own separate identity, it is important to bear in mind that the relationship between the two sections has always been an amicable and friendly one. The story of the ladies section, though not dating back quite as far as the men, can be traced back to just before the First World War.

Indeed, the A. G. M of February 1913 lists the first lady member as Miss A. Goacher, but exactly who this person was remains a mystery, because the Goacher family consisted of Harry, Delia, Dora, Margi and Ruth. Ironically, the following year Miss A. Goacher was replaced by D. Goacher, which was probably Delia. After this there is no more record of the women mentioned in the club minutes until 1922.

It would appear that a short time after the end of the Great War, a number of the Artisans wives decided it was time to have their own club, after all, women had just gained the vote, so it made sense to have their own Artisan section too. The instigators of this were a group of women who were to be the bedrock of the club for the next forty years.

These women were Gwen Steadman, Janet Twibell, Edith Bowles, Delia Goacher and Vivian Jacobs. However, it was Gwen Steadman who approached the then Artisan President, George Denton, to ask if a ladies section could be formed. Denton agreed, and thus the first lady Artisan club came in to being. It is believed that only one other such section was formed and that was at Brancaster in Norfolk, the birthplace of the Jacobs family. Having achieved their objective they quickly moved in to action by joining the Ladies Golf Union in 1926, thereby becoming the first Artisan members.

Although this gives the impression that they were well organised, the level of play was not particularly sophisticated. Indeed, during the early years, few of the ladies had many clubs, none of them had any lockers where they could store their equipment, and it was not an uncommon sight to see the ladies riding their bikes to the course with their clubs over their shoulders. The clubs were often "hand me downs", but as time progressed others were bought from the professional's shop on credit. Some of the ladies also bought their clubs from Suggs sports shop in Sheffield, again on a credit basis. By the time the ladies had overcome the equipment and transportation hurdles they were faced by rules that were quite restrictive.

The playing conditions were determined by the rules that had been drawn up by the Sheffield and District Golf Club in 1922. Essentially, they were restricted to twenty members and they could only play between Monday and Friday. Also of interest were the times at which some of the members could play. Vivian Jacobs, the wife of the club professional, Bob Jacobs, was also the stewardess and could normally only play in the mornings. Quite often she would be seen playing a match before midday, while in the afternoon she would be found preparing lunch for the Lindrick members, and it was for this that she was to became rightly famous.

The ladies, like their male counterparts, were strongly supported by the Parent Club. Indeed, one of the first benefactors was Lady Bingham, wife of Sir Albert Bingham, who graciously donated a trophy for annual competition. First played for in 1928, the Lady Bingham Cup was won by Vivian Jacobs, and is still competed for today. Like the Presidents Bowl and the Leng Cup, the Bingham Cup was also a very competitive affair. The matches were often close and usually fought out between the best players in the club. The 1932 final was no exception when Janet Twibell narrowly defeated Gwen Steadman 2 and 1.

Apart from cups and trophies the ladies also played for various prizes donated by Lindrick Lady Members. In August 1930 a bogey competition was played for Mrs Willis' prize which was won by Vivian Jacobs with a score of 2 up. Mrs Puches also gave a prize, which was a cake basket and this was played for over four rounds of medal during the summer of 1932, when a net score of 318 compiled by Gwen Steadman was good enough to beat Mrs Rowbottom by one shot.

The ladies also took part in individual competitions played at other clubs. In September 1932 Worksop Golf Club held its first Ladies Open Meeting. The competition was a great success, as the words of the Worksop Guardian testify:

"Ideal conditions prevailed, there was a splendid entry, the course was in perfect condition and the scoring was low".

Gwen Steadman had entered from the Artisans, and in the morning medal lost out to Mrs Walmsley from Renishaw by two strokes who shot a net 68. Not exactly content with finishing a gallant second, the afternoon was taken up with a bogey competition where Gwen again finished second on 2 down, losing out this time to Mrs A. Bell from Mickleover who finished 1 down.

Team matches were just as important to the ladies as they were to the men, but during the 1930's they did not achieve the level of success that the men did. However, not that this overly mattered, as the net result was to build successful relationships with other clubs.

Matches were played against the ladies from Worksop Golf Club during the 1930's and in the main the Worksop ladies were triumphant. On May 26th 1930, for example, the ladies lost at Lindrick by 4 matches to 1. Only Gwen Steadman was successful, whilst halves were gained by Vivian Jacobs, Janet Twibell and Mrs Foulds. By the mid 1930's the ladies started to reduce the deficits, until they tied four matches each in June 1933. At last, in May 1934, the Artisans won by 5 1/2 to 2 1/2. Of some interest was the fact that the Artisan team was nearly always composed of the same players, but on this particular day a Miss K. Pickering took to the field. A few years later Miss Pickering was to marry Harry Spencer, one of the Spencer twins and remain a member until 1983. Today, her son, Keith continues the family's association with the club.

Other matches were also played. Lindrick ladies were regularly entertained, but again the Sheffield and District club tendered to be victorious. Better luck though was had against Rother Vale when in June 1933, at Lindrick, the Artisans won by 7 matches to 1. Astonishingly Vivian Jacobs lost!

The ladies of the club were very fortunate in the 1920's and 1930's because they were in a very privileged position. Apart from being one of only two lady artisan clubs in England, they were supported by the parent club on the one hand, while on the other by several prominent members of the men's club, which included Tom Neal and Harry Goacher. In the years directly before the Second World War the ladies section became stronger and stronger and the relationship between the sections became galvanised at both a playing and social level. After the war this foundation was to be invaluable in the development of the club.

CHAPTER 10
ARTISANS AT WAR 1939-1945

On September 1st 1939 Hitler's armies streamed across the German frontier launching a blitzkrieg attack on a helpless Poland that was a surprise to no one. Two days later, at precisely 11 A. M., Britain and France declared war on Germany. It was to be six years before peace was restored and Hitler's armies smashed. The Artisans were to play a role in this, some were to pay the ultimate price with their lives, while others lived to tell the tale, but throughout these traumatic years it was still possible for some members at least to continue playing their favouite game.

Mobilisation of the Artisans was quite slow in the Autumn of 1939, but the club had started to make a contribution by assisting the Parent Club whose ground staff had been reduced. It was also agreed that funds be raised in aid of the Red Cross and on Saturday 2nd December, a whist drive was held that raised the grand sum of £5.

At the A. G. M, just a few days later, it was unanimously agreed that any member serving with His Majesty's Forces would not have to pay their subscription, but those who were likely to be called up, (yet still at home by 26th January 1940), would have to pay. However, the meeting, on the proposition of Leonard Kipling, seconded by Arthur Foulds, stated clearly that:

"By doing so their membership should be reserved for the duration of the war and that they should have the right to play and compete in competitions when at home."

It was clear by September 1940, that the war was going to last much longer than many people expected. The Artisans had tried to continue with organised golf, but due to the circumstances, this was proving very difficult. It seemed to make sense to play matches that aided the war effort, rather than normal club competitions, so on June 1st just days before the army was forced to withdraw from the beaches at Dunkirk, the whole proceeds of the News of the World Medal were donated to the Artisan Golfers Red Cross Appeal. In addition, 10s was sent to the Sheffield Union Red Cross, as Henry Cotton, twice a winner of the Open Championship before the war, was visiting.

As the military situation worsened throughout 1940 and British cities, including Sheffield, were subject to a series of bombing raids, the A. G. M held on 7th December agreed that:

"In view of the prevailing circumstances and the results of competitions during the past season, it was agreed no competitions should be played during 1941."

In addition, it was agreed that all members serving with the forces be given 5s out of club funds. It was a generous offer and represented once again the kind and caring nature of the club to its members.

Roy Kipling on the 1st tee at Meiktilla.
Owned by Roy Kipling.

The club minutes after 1940 tell very little of any golfing activities. The only significant entry was made in 1944 when it was stated that Jack Colton had been killed in action with his unit, the North Staffordshire Regiment, at Normandy a few days after the D-Day landings. The club decided to send a letter of condolence to his mother, Martha, who was the sister of Leonard Kipling.

It is easy to suppose that no golf was played after 1940, but this would be a mistake. The Artisans were not about to allow Hitler to interfere with their golf. Roy Kipling, for example, had been called up in 1944 when he joined the York's and Lanc's Regiment, and was sent to Burma.

It was here, at the end of the Pacific war, that the British Army decided to build its own nine hole course on scrub land to the south of Mandalay. The greens were "browns", the tees were made from earth and stones covered with a bituminous substance and the clubs and balls were purchased from the NAAFI. The balls were not of very good quality and would barely last the nine holes. By the same token the "bag" consisted of just three clubs, so in many ways the game was being played in a similar manner to that of the previous century.

Lurking on the course to menace the competitors were not the usual array of bunkers and water hazards, but just the natural hazards of the time. More often than not these hazards could run, fly and crawl! It was, therefore, always a good idea to check what was in the hole before retrieving your ball. Britain, renowned for the vagaries in its weather, had a strong competitor in Burma which was subject to heavy rains during the monsoon season. When the rain came the course was largely washed away and had to be rebuilt. This proved interesting, as it was a different course every time.

Roy Kipling as successful winner of The Shield at the army golf course at Meiktilla, south of Mandalay, 1946.
Owned by Roy Kipling

The main competition was the Shield which was a foursome and normally competed for as a stableford under handicap. Like many things, it was a serious affair. Suffice to say the trophy was won by Roy and his partner, Ron Bocking, who to this day remains a keen golfer at the Hillsborough Golf Club in Sheffield. An interesting foot note to all this was the fact that the "club" had its own professional who was a Japanese prisoner of war!

Also Roy's uncle, Harry Kipling, had, during the early 1920's been the Assistant Professional at Lindrick, but had moved on to Southport and Ainsdale Golf Club, on the Lancashire coast by the late 20's. As the threat of war increased during 1939, Harry volunteered to join the army, and was posted to Java in Indonesia, where he was captured by the Japanese. Tragically, Harry died in captivity during 1943, whilst working on the Burma to Siam railway.

Nearer to home other members were posted to various parts of the country. Ellis Colton, for example, had joined the 156th (Lanarkshire Yeomanry) Field RA and had been posted to Lanark in Scotland. Feeling a little "golf sick" Ellis wrote home asking for his golf clubs be sent north forthwith. They were duly despatched, the sickness went away and the spare hours were whiled away playing golf at Lesmahagow and Strathaven, which was the home course of the singer and comedian Sir Harry Lauder. In August 1940, when it looked like Hitler was going to invade Great Britain, Ellis' unit was transferred to the Home Army and based on the Isle of White. In the event, due to the heroics of the R.A.F., Hitler was forced to abandon Operation Sealion. It was in these circumstances that it was possible for Ellis to play some more golf at a club near Ryde.

Meanwhile, back at Lindrick, other members were being called up. To write about them all would be a book in itself, but a few examples give an illustration of their exploits and their bravery. George Merrick served throughout the war and fought gallantly at Dunkirk, North Africa, Italy and Western Europe. Alan Spencer, who was a Lindrick employee, served in Malta during the siege, whilst his brother, Harold, spent some time with the territorials, serving in North Africa, Italy, and Western Europe. Sam, Doug and Jack Inman all served abroad. Doug Allen went to North Africa and fought with the 7th Armoured Brigade, The Desert Rats, and Terrence Gillatt was badly wounded late in the war. Finally, Norman Tyson joined the Northamptonshire's, Colin Taylor became a paratrooper and Jack Clarkson joined the R.A.F. All served with distinction.

Those who worked in the mines and in agriculture were excused military service due to their importance to the war effort. Many of these men joined the Home Guard. Two members who fell in to this category were Roy Rowett and his good friend Jack "Staffy" Lion. Often keeping watch over the course in case any enemy aircraft or parachutists tried to land, many hours were whiled away at the lookout shelter that was sited on the right hand side of the thirteenth hole at the top of the hill. On one particular occasion, when there was a very heavy air raid on Sheffield and the sky was full of planes dropping their bombs on the city, it was natural to take cover. As the two friends sheltered, Jack realised that he had left his rifle on top of the corrugated iron roof and said to Roy, somewhat hesitantly, "I'd better get my rifle". Roy replied, "And tha'd better get mine too!" It was one of those lighter moments that was to break the tension. Eventually the raid passed over and the two chums could relax.

During the war the course changed significantly. The Sheffield and District clubhouse was taken over as a maternity hospital and the clubhouse moved to the pavilion that encompassed the professionals shop. On the course itself old cars and trucks were positioned in strategic areas, not to add extra playing hazards, but to stop enemy aircraft from landing on the fairways.

This made the maintenance of the course very interesting. The ground staff was quite depleted by 1940, but several young Artisans filled the void. These were Alan Taylor, George Spencer, who was to remain part of the green staff until his early death in 1967, and Harold Colton, the younger brother of Ellis and Jack. Also part of the staff was Walter Kipling, but he was not an Artisan. Tragedy was to strike this small bunch of friends, when in 1944, Harold Colton left the group to join the Duke of Wellingtons Regiment, and died in service. This was a double blow for the Colton family as Jack Colton had been killed earlier the same year.

Due to petrol rationing, motorised mowing was not allowed and instead the fairways were cut by two gang mowing machines that were pulled by two horses called Jerry and Prince. In addition, there were three or four hand mower's that were used on the greens. The club did have a motorised truck, but this was sold to a motor salesman called Brook. All the clubs provisions were transported by horse and cart and this included coal for the fires that was brought from Shireoaks colliery.

By the Summer of 1945 the war was over. The atomic bombs which had been dropped on Japan ushered in a new age. It was time for the Artisans to do the same. Much needed to be done. In particular drastic work was required on the clubhouse, trophies and cups needed to be located and competitions reorganised.

Part 2
1946-1999

CHAPTER 11
SORTING OUT THE MESS 1946-51

The world in 1945 was a very different one to that which had been left behind in 1939 when W.W.II had broken out. Britain was victorious, yet exhausted. The next few years were to be very difficult as rationing continued and rebuilding began.

If this was true of the nation as whole it was also true of the Artisans as well. The war had exacted its toll and there was much to be done. Jack Clarkson, who had been Honorary Secretary since the early 1930's, summarised the main problems at the end of 1945 in his Secretary's Report as noted below.

- The 1945 season was very disappointing "due in no small measure to many of the boys being in uniform".
- There was no National Tournament in 1945 due to lack of food, accommodation, travelling difficulties, and no suitable course.
- Of the two competitions played in 1945 both were poorly attended. This was due to bad weather on the one hand and the competitors not having any balls on the other!
- Team matches, though discussed with Halifax (Ogden), Buxton, Beauchief, and Tinsley, did not take part due to similar reasons as the National Tournament.
- The Clubhouse was in a dilapidated state.

The Presidency of the Artisans in 1946 had passed to Geoffrey Gullick, who along with Jack Clarkson set about the business of sorting out the mess. The first issue was that of adopting a set of rules governing the running of the club. Though this may have been seen as less than a priority, it was important because it formalised many of the "gentleman's agreements" made since the last set of rules were issued in 1912.

Jack Clarkson and the Committee did the majority of the work, and when completed in 1948 passed them to the Parent Club for approval. The main points were that:

- An honorarium of £25 per annum was to be paid to Lindrick

Golf Club for the courtesy of the course.
- That the qualifying area for application be Woodsetts, Shireoaks, and Turnerwood.
- That the total membership be 90, comprising of 70 males and 20 females.
- The qualifying age to be 16.
- Elected officials to run the business of the club, through an elected committee.
- Provision for an Annual General Meeting and Special General Meeting.
- Rules governing the sale of intoxicating beverages, as required by the Licensing Acts.
- And a code of conducts governing playing conditions.

Though these rules have been modified over the years, they have remained essentially the same. With a firm foundation now in place it was time to move on.

The state of the clubhouse left much to be desired. Essentially, it was just a wooden shed, which had been converted from an open garage that had been used by the chauffeurs of the Sheffield and District Golf Club. It was hardly comfortable, had few amenities, though electricity had been fitted in the 1930's, and it was largely impossible to entertain guests or hold effective meetings. The war years had made matters worse, as it had been impossible to repair any damage or plan modifications.

For these reasons the Annual General Meeting and committee meetings were often held elsewhere. For example the 1947 A.G.M was held at the Station Hotel at Shireoaks, and was normally followed by the club dinner and social evening. This was an effective move as this tendered to increase the attendance. Meanwhile, committee meetings were held in Woodsetts School, Woodsetts Church Institute or at George Herrington's cottage located behind the first tee.

Due to the war building materials were scarce, and like food, were rationed on the basis of priority. Financial consideration was also important, and there was little money available to commence grandiose projects. Nevertheless, it was decided to make improvements where possible, so in June 1947 it was decided to approach the

Sheffield and District Golf Club with a view to having running water connected, and "if permission be granted an estimate of the cost obtained".

Permission was obtained from the Parent Club, as well as from the Kiveton Park Rural District Council, who on completion would ratify the work. W. Wright's quotation of £65 was quickly accepted. This covered the plumbing, the installation of the main, supplying all pipes and inspection covers, and also included all the bricks and cement. The excavation of the trenches was to be completed by voluntary labour, and the work to commence on 22nd March 1948.

Unfortunately, the project did not run very smoothly, and by June the job was still unfinished. The main issue was the pipe track, and to make matters worse Kiveton Park Rural District Council had condemned the work so far completed. Infact, things were so bad that they said "if the meter chamber is not built in within ten days, we will do same, and charge it to the club."

In the end a new contractor, Earle and Proberts, completed the work at the additional cost of £17/1/3, who were then asked to look at the heating of the club by building a rustic fireplace. A quote for £10 was approved, but like Wright's before them, Earle and Proberts let the club down and the work remained unfinished until April 1949, when it was decided to re-tender the contract to E. Sims. The future was going to be much better, but for the moment the Artisans had to make the best of it. From a golfing point of view things slowly got back to normal, with all the pre-war competitions being played as before.

One of the strongest players in this period was Alan Spencer, who was a member of the green staff. With a swing that was the envy of many, he dominated both 1946 and 1947 by winning the Leng Cup, Kayser Cup, and Challenge Cup (twice) as well as the Commonside Foursomes. The other dominating player at this time was Jack Clarkson, whose prodigious strength helped him to win three of the major club titles during 1947 and 1948. At the same time a new force in the playing ranks was emerging, when William "Bill" Randall and Jim Merrick won the Kayser Cup in 1950 and 1951. During the 50's these two men became the leading players of the club, and the standard by which everyone else measured themselves.

The highlight in this period however, were the victories gained by

Ellis Colton and Norman Tyson in the Sheffield Telegraph Cup and Trophy. These competitions had been played since 1924 and were open to all amateur players, playing within a twenty-five mile radius of Sheffield, with handicaps of eight or less for the Telegraph Cup, while those with handicaps above eight competed for the Telegraph Trophy.

In the summer of 1946, while rationing was still in force, Norman Tyson decided to enter the Telegraph Trophy that was being played at the Hallowes Golf Club in Sheffield. Paying an entrance fee of 7 shillings, and from a handicap of 17, Norman scored 72, 71 for 143, which was good enough to finish in a three way tie with A. S. Jackson and S. Berisford both of Lees Hall. Norman gained victory by virtue of having the best back nine on the last round. Undoubtedly pleased, Norman received the trophy from Councillor F. H. Price, who was President of the Sheffield Union of Golf Clubs.

The day was significant for another reason. Ellis Colton also played and finished in eighth place with a score of 151, but he also won a prize for the best first round gross of 83. By 1947 Ellis had improved his game sufficiently to enter the prestigious Telegraph Cup, which was being played at Lindrick on Saturday 28th June over two rounds of medal.

Richard Sparling of the Sheffield Telegraph describes how the twenty-seven year old colliery clerk from Firbeck had been practising every night for two weeks for the event, yet though "an occasional six crept on to his cards...he was never in serious trouble. Colton has learnt the value of straightness at Lindrick". With net scores from eight handicap of 71, 73 for

Sheffield Telegraph Cup held at Lindrick in 1947.
Owned by Ellis Colton.

a total of 144 Ellis was victorious by one shot from J. Kennedy, a former English schoolboy international, and Harry Bates the Honorary Secretary of Tinsley Park Golf Club. Horace Merrick, who also played, finished eighth. At the end of the tournament the Lindrick Captain G. M. Gullick, who during his presentation speech commented on the high standard of the course and the quality of the competitors, presented the Cup to Ellis and the prizes to the runners up.

It was a great way to forget about the post war deprivations and look to the future. From Ellis Colton's point of view it was the fulfilment of a family ambition that had begun before the war, as his father William and his cousin Charles, had both narrowly missed victory in the past. The 1950's were nearly upon the club. It was to be a decade of unbridled success and great satisfaction, as the combination of playing conditions, clubhouse comforts and golfing prowess all blended perfectly together.

CHAPTER 12
GOLF IN THE 50'S

The 1950's were, on reflection, probably the best decade the club ever had. Indeed, not only could Harold Macmillan say, "you've never had it so good", but the Artisans could say the same too. There were during this time some very gifted players like William "Bill" Randall, Horace and Jim Merrick, Norman Tyson, Jim Oldale, Alan Spencer, Jim Highfield and Roy Kipling, whose handicaps were in the three to five range, and who were very competitive with it. But perhaps more importantly, there was another group of players in the mid range handicaps that formed the real strength of the club, men such as Ellis Colton, Len Morris, George Robinson, Oscar Clarkson and Doug Allen to mention but a few.

Lindrick Artisan members 1950. Left to right top. Jim Oldale, Jack Jacobs, Arnold Knowles, Tony Barker (L.G.C), George Herrington, G.M. Gullick (President), Frank Stothard, Oscar Clarkson, A.S. Furniss (L.G.C). Bottom left to right. David Snell, Peter Allen, Roy Kipling, Jack Hall, Harry Pollard, Wilf Hall, Joe Mee, Leonard Kipling.

Owned by Alan Taylor.

The start of the decade was very quiet, as the old competitions continued as before. Importantly though the Artisans started to play more at other courses. This was due in part to easier transport and the growth of inter-club competitions. As mentioned previously, one of the most popular of these tournaments was the Sheffield Telegraph Trophy. Norman Tyson had won this in 1946 and competed most years. Indeed, having won in 1946 he came fifth in a tie with Harold Brewer the following year. In 1952 the competition was held on Saturday June 21st at Wheatley Golf Club at Doncaster, where Norman shot 68,70 for a total of 138, which was good enough to beat David Lindsay, (the Scottish back of Barnsley Football Club), by three shots. It was unique because no one had ever won the title twice. Richard Sparling of the Sheffield Telegraph wrote, "His driving was long and rarely off line, and his putting consistently good."

Back at Lindrick the business of competitions continued. There was however, some dispute as to what constituted a competition, and with it the determination of handicaps. This question was prompted by the News of the World Medal in 1950, when due to bad weather there were only six entries. In future it was decided that a minimum of twelve entries would be necessary to constitute a competition, otherwise it would be deemed null and void. At the same time it was decided that a rota would be worked out for all future competitions. Handicapping, which was always a contentious issue, had for many years been at the purview of the general committee. The process invariably took up much valuable committee time, so it was decided to form a separate committee to specifically manage the process.

Another issue of some debate was the process involved in choosing a club Captain. Before the war the Captain was largely the head of the Committee, and referred to as Chairman. It was not uncommon for a member to be Chairman several times, and both Harry Goacher and R. O. Spencer held this position eight and four times respectively. After the war circumstances had changed. Now most clubs were electing club captains who acted as the figurehead of the club, the issue was how to elect them. Thus, at the 1953 A.G.M it was agreed that a meeting of past-captains would be held to select a vice-captain for the following season. Though no stipulation was made to how many past-captains should make up the meeting, it was stated that no less than four must be present to decide a nominee. In-fact, the system was so good that in 1998 the method remained unchanged.

By the early 1950's the club was still playing for the same prizes and trophies as before the war. Either the President or the Vice-Presidents donated many of these prizes. Jack Ridgway, who had taken over as President in 1949 from Geoffrey Gullick, donated a prize of a box of tools for the all season eclectic. This prize was much sought after by the Artisans, but this was only one of many. This was to change however during the late 1950's. The first change came in 1955 when the competition Secretary suggested that either the Leng Cup or the Kayser Cup should be known as the Club Championship. After a little debate it was decided that the Leng Cup should have the honour and it was agreed that the competition be played over 36 holes on a Sunday late in the golfing year. In addition it was also decided that those who could not play in competitions on Saturday could play on a Thursday. This principle stayed in place for nearly thirty years until it became against the rules of golf to play one round of a competition on separate days.

The major change came towards the end of the 1950's when the club acquired two new trophies. The first of these was the George Harrison Trophy, which was established in 1956. George was one of the older members of the club, and had recently been nominated for honorary membership, and decided to donate a trophy to the club as a mark of gratitude. The trophy was received with thanks, but disaster was to strike when it was dropped by accident and broke. What caused so much consternation was that it found to be made of clay, much to the embarrassment of all concerned. Fortunately, a replica was commissioned and is still played for today.

In 1957 George Hallam died. He was another long serving member of the club, and his son Robert, asked if he could donate a trophy to be played for in memory of his father. This was duly accepted and played for over one round of medal with the four best scores qualifying for the knockout stages. Both of these trophies began the start of a process that would over the next thirty years or so lead to more and more cups and prizes being played for. In addition however, the members themselves also donated prizes for specific competitions. Jack Palmer, for example, the butcher from Shireoaks, gave prizes of poultry for the Christmas Fayre competition in 1958, and continued to do so for many years. Other members donated bottles of whisky, for instance, and this proved very popular!

From the playing point of view there is very little surviving information to tell who won what, and what scores they achieved. Most contemporaries of the period would not dispute the fact that Jim Merrick and Bill Randall were the leading players in the club. Both low handicap players in the three to four category, they were fiercely competitive, but above all they were extremely straight hitters. This was very important at the time because the fairways were narrower and the gorse, which was dominant on the course, was much tighter than today. What is known is that in 1957 the Leng Cup was a very tight affair. Normally the low handicap players tended to dominate the competition, but this time is was contested between two high handicap players Jack Palmer and Harry Bedford, 20 and 19 handicap respectively. After two rounds they were both tied on 150, but Jack was deemed the winner by virtue of having a better last round of 73 to Harry's 76. Infact, Jack Palmer had quite a good year as along with Jack Clarkson, he also won Mr Stephen Wild's Prize.

The Captain in 1957 was Jack Hall, and the winner of Captains Day was George Robinson with a score of 3up on bogey, while in second place was nine handicapper Harold Brewer and five handicapper Alan Spencer who both finished 1 down. Also of interest was the fact that there was a junior division for the high handicap players and this was won by R. O. Spencer who also finished 1 down.

One other interesting point to survive was the experience of George Merrick in the spring of 1958. Playing the 11th at Lindrick, with his two brothers Jim and Horace, he was lucky enough to hole his tee shot, yet extraordinarily he repeated the feat at the 18th hole at Worksop a few days later!

The 1950's were good years for the Artisans as the club really came of age. Its players were competent, and with largely unrestricted golf, some were exceptional. Other chapters tell of their exploits at the northern tournament and in team matches, but for the moment everything was running very smoothly on the "common".

CHAPTER 13
CLUB AFFAIRS 1946-70

In the immediate post-war period the country had elected a new government, whose mandate it was to build a new modern Britain: and in the same way Clement Attlee's Labour Party had many difficulties to overcome, so the Artisans had a number of matters to attend to also. A previous chapter has discussed this in some detail, but as an example Committee meetings were either held in Woodsetts School, or at the George Herrington's cottage at the back of the first tee, as the clubhouse was in a state of disrepair. Yet there were other matters requiring attention by both the committee and the club officials.

In 1946 the officers of the club comprised of Jack Clarkson who was Honorary Secretary, George Herrington who was Honorary Match Secretary, while his uncle, Sam Herrington, was Honorary Treasurer. Sam, who had been one of the founder members in 1899, and Treasurer since at least 1924, and possibly 1912, had in recent years begun to suffer from ill health. Indeed, the result of this was that he began to lose touch with what was happening in the club, and it became increasingly difficult for the Secretary and the Treasurer to communicate on matters of importance. The issue reached a head in 1947, when at the A.G.M, Harry Goacher spoke in some detail about the difficulties that were being experienced. At the end of the debate the meeting agreed to elect Harry Goacher to the position of Treasurer with immediate effect. As in 1930, when Jack Clarkson became Secretary, a watershed had been reached, but Harry Goacher was keen to emphasise that:

"He had not brought up this matter with this office in mind, and requested that a letter be sent to Sam Herrington thanking him for his past services."

Over the next few years there were a number of appointments to the position of Match Secretary, as both Ellis Colton and Arnold Knowles held the post. Yet it was the position of the Treasurer that seemed to be the key to stability. Harry Goacher relinquished the post in 1953, due ironically to the problem of communication with Jack

Clarkson. Arnold Knowles took up the position, and since both he and Jack worked in Worksop it was far easier for decisions to be made. This created a vacancy to the Match Secretary's position that was taken by Roy Kipling. For the next twenty-one years this triumvirate held the senior positions in the club, and apart from one challenge to Jack Clarkson's position of Secretary by Ellis Colton, they were largely unopposed.

During this period subscriptions were still very moderate, as the annual honorarium to Lindrick Golf Club remained largely a token of good will. Thus, in 1947 subscriptions were 10/6d. However, by 1948 post war austerity forced the club to consider helping Lindrick Golf Club by increasing the honorarium to £25 per annum, whilst also assisting with the purchase of specialist feeds for the course. Indeed, the President, G.M. Gullick, said at the 1948 A.G.M that Lindrick Golf Club finances were not as good as they had been in 1939. Not surprisingly, the Artisans rallied to the cause: a theme that has been prevalent down the years.

However, the club subscription rose dramatically as a result in 1948 to £1, which was nearly double the figure for 1947! Over the next twenty years the figure increased steadily as prices rose and the aspirations of the club increased. During the late 1960's this increase accelerated so that in 1969 subscriptions stood at £5. Nevertheless, this figure still represented excellent value for money, on one of the best golf courses anywhere in the country.

Meanwhile, the running of the club continued in other ways. In the early '40's and '50's the club A.G.M, Dinner and Prize Presentation were combined. Various venues were chosen including the Station Hotel at Shireoaks, and the Golden Ball at Worksop. The combination of these two functions tended to ensure a good attendance, but generally they were all male affairs. In 1947, for example, the 5/6d menu was chosen, and the Sharpe Brothers of Whitwell, as well as an impressionist were engaged to provide the entertainment. In addition a special bus was organised to convey the members to and from the Golden Ball.

In 1949 the ladies were invited to the dinner, but prices had increased to 6/6d or 12/ per couple, while James and Harry Scaife, who had been recommended by Doug Inman, provided the entertainment. A great night was had by all, and the ladies Secretary, Janet Twibell, took the opportunity of thanking the men for inviting them to the dinner for the first time and hoped it would not be the last.

Nevertheless, the functions during this period, though successful, were not exactly solvent. Surprisingly some significant losses were made that were largely attributable to the cost of hiring professional entertainers. Losses in 1947 and 1948 were £6/5/0 and £5/8/0 respectively, while in 1950 it was £4/8/6d. After a further loss of £3/9/0 was made in 1950 the Committee agreed "that these functions should be made to pay for themselves."

In 1952 it was decided that the prize presentation and dinner should be held separately from the A.G.M, and it has remained this way ever since. The venue for the dinner, which had become established in recent years at the Golden Ball, was unavailable, so the restaurant of the Co-operative Society was engaged instead. It was asignificant moment as the dinner was to be held here for over twenty years. Interestingly the cost of the meal was 6/ but guests were charged 7/6d to cover costs, a shrewd move considering previous losses, yet the dinner still lost £7/19/0! For most of the decade this style of arrangement continued, but like all things the members started to lose interest and a fresh approach was required.

This initiative came from Arnold Knowles who proposed an Artisan version of the popular television programme "This is Your Life." Based on the members the series was a great success, though whether Eammon Andrews knew much about it is uncertain! Following the same format as the television the programme, all the preparation was done beforehand, and no one knew who was going to be the lucky person, but Arnold managed to catch unawares Jack Jacobs, Doug Allen, Bill Taylor, Tommy Widdison, Jack Clarkson, and George Merrick. When the "victim" was known no one was allowed to leave the room, until Arnold had closed his Red Book.

This change spurred the event on, and in 1960 a sketch on the American Curtis Cup team was performed, when Jack Palmer, Horace Merrick and others dressed up in drag at the dinner. A further initiative was tried when the younger members were encouraged to participate in the entertainment as well. At the time when popular music was catching everyone's attention, Roger Merrick, Clive Betts,

Curtis Cup Team 1960 - Artisan style. Len Morris, Jack Palmer, Horace Merrick, ColinTaylor, Doug Inman, Doug Allen, Gordon Swift, Eric Taylor, and Arnold Knowles.

Owned by Arnold Knowles.

David Spencer and Trevor Dinsdale became the "Lindrick Beatles" which was received to rapturous applause. It was simple fun based on the concert party format that was familiar to the clubs ex-servicemen and women.

However, by the end of the 1960's even this had run its course, and the sub-committee on entertainment "decided to abandon the idea of professional entertainment" as the "younger members of the club...wished to be entertained not entertain."

Other aspects of the club were under review at this time. Club rules, for example, had changed little from those that had been adopted by the club in 1948, but ad hoc adjustments were made. Some of these changes simply consolidated existing practices, while others accounted for previous oversights. Thus, a special meeting called on Christmas Day 1949 lowered the qualification age to 16! The decision was unanimous and forwarded to Lindrick Golf Club for final approval, which was granted in January 1950.

1953 saw the issue of non-playing members. This was a category of people who did not fit in to the group who would normally be eligible for honorary membership, but who wanted to enjoy the day to day privileges of the club. After much discussion it was decided to fix this at no more than twenty, and confine them to ex-playing members. After Lindrick Golf Club approved this, the subscription was fixed at 2/6d. However, in the event, only ten members were elected.

The late 1950's and '60's saw some minor changes to the eligibility criteria of prospective members. In the 1930's four Dinington men had tried to join the club, but were excluded on the grounds that they resided outside the qualifying area. In 1957 the issue rose its head again when Anston Parish Council tried to get twenty parishioners elected to the club. Lindrick Golf Club had established since the 1930's that only the residents of Woodsetts, Shireoaks, and Turnerwood qualified for membership to the Artisans: yet part of the course lay within the Anston parish boundary. Not unnaturally this caused some resentment, but Lindrick Golf Club met the Anston council to discuss the matter. Colonel J. Sorby represented Lindrick Golf Club at the meeting and asured the Anston councillors that their request would be considered carefully, but after due consideration the applications were refused nevertheless. Thus, in 1959 it was decided to require prospective members to have resided in one of the three villages for a minimum of one year before being eligible for membership, while in the 1960's it was agreed that "members sons and local born persons should receive first consideration." The issue was certainly uppermost in the minds of many Lindrick Golf Club members, when Sir Wilton-Lee expressed:

"The Parent Club's concern about the growth of the locality, and the way Lindrick may be regarded."

For the moment the issue subsided, but in the 1970's Anston Parish Council campaigned once again for their residents to be considered for membership of the Artisans.

As the club grew, so did the members aspirations, and with it the management of the associated responsibilities. Prior to the war, the club was a very simple affair, but soon afterwards this was to change.

Alcoholic beverages had only been available in bottles, (there was no bar), and technically the sale of such beverages was illegal. In the immediate post war periods, as the clubhouse was re-built, so bar facilities were added, and with it came the necessity to acquire a beer licence. Thus, in 1949 the committee instructed Jack Clarkson to "engage a private solicitor for such purpose". This was duly done for the royal sum of £3/13/6d!

Now set on a proper footing the bar prospered, and although profits were modest this all helped in the financial running of the club. However, not everything was as smooth running as it seemed. An oversight in early 1962 caused the bar to be "officially dry" for two months, as the 1961 Licensing Act required the club to re-register. Fortunately normal service was resumed in July 1962, and since then there has not been a repeat of the same mistake! Yet the cost of the mistake was £16/17/0 in solicitors fees.

The advent of the bar and major improvements in the comforts of the clubhouse encouraged the members to use the facilities increasingly for social events. These were normally modest: whist drives being one example, but other more ambitious ideas were to follow. One of the most interesting ones were the film's that were shown in the 1960's. The first was held in 1962 when a holiday film was hired from Woodcock Travel in Worksop about Canada. To show it the club borrowed a projector from the Steetley Company.

Over the next few years other films were hired. Not unnaturally these included ones about golf, and in 1965 the club showed the highlights of the 1964 Piccadilly World Matchplay Championship final, when Neil Coles played the great Arnold Palmer. This film was very popular indeed. 1966 saw the Dunlop Masters film shown which was particularly liked as it was played at Lindrick. By the end of the decade these events were still well attended, and were to continue for some years afterwards.

The growth of the club did unfortunately attract some attention it did not want. On several occasions during the 1950's and 1960's the club was burgled. The first occasion was in 1954 when the total loss was estimated at £14/15/0. The second incidence was in September 1962 when goods were taken from the bar valued at £19. This included £3/10 in cash, bottles of spirits, and cigarettes. This prompted discussion on the fitting of a burglar alarm, but nothing was actually done.

Unfortunately, worse was to follow in 1968 when wines and spirits were taken valued at £24/7/7, cigarettes at £26/11/1, a record player at £18 and three boxes of Black Magic Chocolates! In addition the clubs of Roy Kipling and Jack Stocks were also taken. Where no one had been caught in the past better luck was to follow this time when the thieves were caught and put in Armley prison at Leeds! Having been bitten twice in recent times the committee decided to fit extra mortice locks to the inner doors, and add iron bars to the windows. The clubs were returned, but one bag and accessories were not. The insurance company was feeling particularly generous and offered £3 in compensation!

Generally speaking this was a very good time for the Artisans as the club grew not only in playing stature but also socially too. Under the guidance of Jack Clarkson and the Committee much was achieved: it was the best of times.

CHAPTER 14
A CLUB TO RIVAL ALL OTHERS
1951-1962

At the end of 1949 Geoffrey Gullick stepped down as President, and Jack Ridgway, who was Chairman of Ridgway Tools in Sheffield, took over. He was to be President for the next twelve years, and along with Jack Clarkson, was destined to transform the club.

Some work had been done in the post war years, but financial limitations on the one hand and building constraints on the other had tendered to hamper matters. This was to change radically in the 1950's, as Lindrick Artisans (as it was to become known in 1956) became a club to rival all others. The reconstruction pro-

Jack Ridgway, President 1949-1962.
Owned by Lindrick Artisans Golf Club.

gramme can be broken down in to three periods 1950-2, 1957-59, and 1962. In-fact, apart from the squaring off of the clubroom in 1974 the club was to remain largely unchanged until the refit of 1998.

The decision to redevelop the clubhouse was taken in November 1950 when the committee agreed to "obtain the advice and estimate of an architect". The first stage was to completely brick in and re-roof the existing building, but since building licenses were still needed it was decided to complete the work in two stages, one pre June 1951 and the other sometime afterwards. The architect engaged was Mr Arthur Clarkson, who was the assistant surveyor with Kiveton Park Rural District Council, and who just happened to live at Deep Carr

Farm, just a short iron from the clubhouse! By the end of 1951 the plans had been submitted to the Parent Club for approval, whilst at the same time the issue of financing the work was also being pondered.

Fortunately, relief was at hand as at the 1951 A. G. M, the Treasurer, Harry Goacher, stated the approximate cost of the extensions, whereupon the President agreed to loan the club £500. All present were shocked by this generosity, and after Harry Goacher had thanked the President all "the members applauded".

As before progress was to be slow due to:

"The Ministry of Works had since stated that owing to the economic situation it was regretted that our alterations could not be included in the 1952 programme, and no license could be granted."

Undaunted, the committee decided to press on and do some of the work anyway, so after discussion with Kiveton Park Rural District Council it was agreed £100 worth of work could be done immediately, and further £100 worth by June 1953.

Work commenced on the lockers, the lavatory areas and brickwork, but funds were running low. It was decided in July 1952 to borrow £500 to complete the building work to the exterior structure, and estimates were tendered by several local builders which included Earl and Probert's, Jackson Brothers, Dernie and Bell, and Hall and Son. In the end the quote of Jackson Brothers for £152/10/0 was accepted, meanwhile the rewiring and fitting of nine new lights and three new power points was undertaken by Mr M. Hughes for the sum of £23/10/0. The plumbing came to £28/18/0, while asbestos for the roof was £29/11/8.

Much excavation work was done for the floors, and it was during this time that a rare artefact was discovered that had lain untouched for the last sixty years. Buried in the earth was a gutta percha golf ball that had been lost sometime at the end of the last century. The find is interesting because the site of the Artisan clubhouse was the location of the old ninth green when the original nine hole course was laid out, and played in the opposite direction to today. Whether or not this ball should reside in a museum is debatable, but for those interested the ball can be seen in the Artisans clubhouse resplendent in its own display case.

By the end of 1952 stage one was largely completed. The club now had a separate locker room and toilet area, as well as an agreeable clubroom, which now included a purpose built bar. At the 1952 A.G.M Harry Goacher thanked all those who had helped to complete the project. Special mention was made of the aid given by the President when he said:

"Without which it would have been impossible for the Artisans to have proceeded with the alterations to the clubroom."

Jack Ridgway was humbled by this gratitude, and asked how much could be re-paid over the next two years. The reply was £200 per year, whereupon the President agreed that he would donate the rest as a gift. The gesture was unanimously approved, and apart from the money owed to the President, only £41 was outstanding to anyone else.

Indeed, the financing of the project was uppermost in everyones mind, and great efforts were made to raise money wherever possible. Whist nights and dances were used to this effect. The Palaise de Danse in Worksop, a popular nightspot at this time, was used in December 1951, whilst several dance and whist drives were held either in Woodsetts school or the Church institute. Meanwhile similar efforts were being held in Shireoaks, which were organised by Fred Marsh who was the postmaster. Of particular interest was the Easter whist drive of 1952 held at Woodsetts School. Table hire was 3d, and water for refreshments and washing was carried from Mrs Rowett's, (Roy Rowett's mother) who lived opposite the school, and who had a copper in which hot water could be boiled! Outside catering had very little meaning in those days.

In addition to this, money was raised by having a Christmas draw, and this was so popular that three hundred extra books had to be printed to meet the demand! At the same time sweepstakes were organised on the St Leger horserace, (which raised £32/10/0), the Grand National, (entry fee 2/6), and the Ebor handicap, raising £11/7/0. For the moment there was a short break until the next phase began.

Stage two commenced in early 1957 after the committee felt that a separate ladies toilet, committee room, and other amenities were required. Jack Clarkson then met the secretary of the Parent club to discuss the matter along with a number of related issues. However, at the end of 1956 the club decided to honour Jack Ridgway for his benevolence to the club over recent years by naming the bar after him. At the 1956 A.G.M Roy Kipling unveiled the new sign above the bar, and the "Ridgway Arms" was open for business. The President appreciated the gesture, and to this day the Ridgway Arms continues to trade, wrapping a consolatory arm around many a vanquished golfer!

In March 1957 Lindrick Golf Club gave permission for the alterations to commence, on the understanding that the following criteria were met.

- All liabilities were the responsibility of the Artisans.
- All rates and taxes were payable by the L.A.G.C.
- All water and electricity charges to be payable by the Artisans.
- Insurance on the premises to be paid by the artisans.
- That the premises be kept in proper repair, with appropriate maintenance where required.

With this clearly understood estimates were put out to obtain the best price. However, not a great deal happened during the rest of 1957, nor indeed 1958, but in September a further estimate was obtained that was £300 cheaper than the rest, but the best price came from Pick and Co. of Ranby, whose price of £1,109/9/8d was accepted.

At the 1958 A.G.M the President once more agreed to give £500 immediately, and £500 later to help complete the work. Arnold Knowles proposed a vote of thanks, while Roy Kipling suggested the President be made a life member. Both were unanimously carried.

By the late summer of 1959 the work was complete, and the grand opening was set for 2p.m on 13th September. It was a very splendid occasion, as it was also Tommy Widdison's Captain's day. Amongst the honoured guests were Sir Stuart Goodwin, the man who had brought the Ryder Cup to Lindrick two years previously, the President, Jack Ridgway, Lindrick Captain, Colonel Dennis Brown, along with other Lindrick guests, Peter Osborn, and W.H.M. Smith, as well as over forty Artisan members.

CHAPTER 15
THE SWINGING 60'S AND THE GLAMOROUS 70'S

The 1960's were a decade of great political and economic change in Britain. In the early years Harold Macmillan was talking about the "wind of change blowing through Africa", while by the late 60's Harold Wilson was saying that "the pound in your pocket" was worth just as much as it had always been. In music the Beatles were top of the pops, and Twiggy was a fashion icon. They were exciting days.

They were also exciting times for the Artisans. A new group of members had joined the club in the late 1950's and early 1960's, injecting youth and ambition in to the game that was in part being driven by the rise of golf as a popular public sport. These men included players such as Brian and Trevor Dinsdale, Roger Merrick, Michael Rowett, Ken Herrington and Clive Betts. It was a new generation for new era. Nevertheless, a new member was not fully accepted, according to the committee, until the Secretary had written "to all new members on what was expected of them in the way of manners, etiquette and discipline."

Making his mark first was Trevor Dinsdale. In 1960, in only his second season, he won the prestigious Leng Cup, a feat he was to repeat in 1969 and 1970, as well as the Commonside Foursomes in partnership with Peter Allen, who was to die tragically three years later. Not to be outdone Clive Betts won both the Leng Cup and the Challenge Cup in 1963, while at the same time the father and son partnership of George and Trevor Dinsdale won the Commonside Foursomes. In the same year that his father was Captain, 1966, Roger Merrick won the Challenge Cup, as did Ken Herrington in 1969. Brian Dinsdale won the Hallam Trophy in 1963, but Michael Rowett had to wait until 1972 before he triumphed in the Spencer Trophy.

The decade saw the introduction of more new trophies to compliment the Hallam and Harrison Trophies that had been introduced in the 1950's. The first of these was the Denton Trophy in 1964. This trophy had originally been donated by George Denton, the first

Flat Caps and Bicycle Clips

Lindrick Artisans Golf Club Prize Presentation 1963. E. A. Barker, President, presenting the Leng Cup to Clive Betts, while Jack Singleton, Roy Kipling, Jack Clarkson, George Dinsdale, Trevor Dinsdale, Ted Blagg and Brian Dinsdale look on.
Owned by Trevor Dinsdale.

president, and had been won outright by Arnold Cawkwell some time in the early 1920's. Handed back in 1964, it has been played for ever since, and was originally decided by the player who recorded the best six medal rounds net. Meanwhile, some members achieved great success away from Lindrick.

In 1965, for instance, Doug Allen played in the Banning Cup, which had been staged at Tinsley Park Golf Club in Sheffield since 1921. In 1922 Arnold Cawkwell had brought the trophy back to Lindrick, but it was to be forty-three years before it returned, when Doug shot two 69's to win. The same year Len Morris, an ardent golfer, won the Area Coal Board Trophy at Worksop Golf Club, while the reliable Ken Widdison took the trophy for the best gross score.

Meanwhile back at Lindrick Frank Stothard won the 1965 Leng Cup, when Ken Herrington, in his first year, needing only a five at the short 18th to win became bunkered, and then three putted to lose. The 1968 competition was also very tight and exciting. Three players were in contention, George Inman, Len Morris, and Jack Clarkson. George lost his ball at the 17th in his second round and could finish no better than a 76 for a two round total of 147. Meanwhile, not far behind was Len Morris, but his challenge came to an end when he went out of bounds at the 16th, and his second round 72 was not quite enough. Jack Clarkson however, needed only to finish with two pars to win, but took two fives instead. So George Inman won the most exciting competition for years!

In 1969 two new trophies appeared. The first of these was the Shireoaks Plate, which was donated by the sister of the late Jack Palmer. He had been the butcher from Shireoaks and a stalwart Artisan member for many years, participating in any event, whether socially or competitively, either home or away. Keen though he was, he was always a high handicap player, and so it was deemed only proper that the lesser players of the club should compete for the new trophy. It was decided that the player who recorded the best three rounds net throughout the season would be the winner.

Jack's legacy though was remembered before this time, however. After his death in 1963 the club decided to honour his memory by playing the Christmas Fayre competition in his name. This was most appropriate as he often donated prizes to the club, which usually consisted of beef and poultry. Catering was also one of his skills as well, as he organised the meal for the match against Lindrick Golf Club from time to time. Indeed, he said providing a hot meal of steak and kidney pie "could be done as cheaply as a cold salad." In the first competition in 1964 the winners were Derek Waterhouse and Derek Singleton who shot a 72, beating the youthful Clive Betts and Cyril Widdison by one shot.

Meanwhile, the Captains Cup was donated by a friend of Roy Rowett, Mervyn Price and two of his colleagues, to be played for by the past captains at the end of the season. In some ways these new trophies filled the void that was being left by the decline in inter-club matches that before the War had been very important.

Another competition that came in to existence was the Presidents Putter. The original idea was to buy an antique putter and adorn it with silver medals and dedicate it to the Christmas Fayre that was very popular at this time. The money was to come from a $20 bill that had been left by the Americans with Jack Jacobs in 1957 after the Ryder Cup. However, Jack Ridgway said that he had an old Braid Mills putter that he believed would meet the requirements outlined.

The Artisans, frugal to a man, accepted the offer and used the $20 to buy the medals on which the winner's names would be inscribed. These medals were bought from Colonel Dennis Brown of the Parent Club at the beginning of January 1962. The putter resides to this day in its own display case, though the competition is no-longer played for, but without its medals as these were unfortunately stolen during a burglary in 1968.

By the late 1960's the nature of golf had changed. Now more popular than ever before, the simple format of club and team matches had changed. Where once club outings and matches were easy to arrange, now it was difficult to find a venue on the one hand and opponents on the other. Most clubs now had other commitments and the relationships that had grown up previously were slowly being lost. Another chapter will discuss these developments, but a fresh approach was required. Most clubs now had Invitation Days, so in August 1967 the Artisans decided to follow suit.

Some 55 members requested to play, making a total of 110 with guests, and as a result the Parent Club was approached and agreed to an early start. The ladies volunteered to run the putting competition, and catering arrangements were organised under the supervision of Mrs Palmer and other lady members. In addition the cost was £1 per member, but the day resulted in a loss of nearly £22 which was borne by the club.

From the golfing point of view everything went perfectly and in a greensome bogey Norman Tyson and his partner E. Robbins finished six up. Five other pairs finished one up, and even the weather was idyllic. As a footnote some caddy carts went missing, one of which belonged to Ellis Colton, and did not re-surface- literally- until the autumn when the pond at the entrance to the club was being cleared! Other rules also applied. Guests had to have an official handicap of twenty or better from either a society or a club.

1968 saw the introduction of the Spencer Trophy, which was

donated by one of the first members R.O. Spencer, in honour of his son George who had died that year. Played originally over the best three rounds of four under medal rules it was a tough test of golf, that relied upon consistency for success. It also carried a prize of £5, which was also a significant motivator.

By the 1970's Ted Heath was taking the country in to the Common Market, and Gary Glitter and the Bay City Rollers were top of the charts. Flares were all the rage, and the long hair that was being worn by some men was causing gender confusion to the older generation!

Captains Day 1971. Doug Inman, John "Maurice" Jacobs, and Harold Brewer on the first tee.

Owned by Bessie Brewer.

Arnold Knowles had proposed in the 1950's that the Captain should be given a grant to help with the purchase of prizes on Captains Day. This idea was accepted, and by 1972 the allowance had reached £30, with the result that more members felt inclined to accept the offer. Further developments occurred in 1966 when the opportunity was taken to invite the Captain of Lindrick Golf Club, Roy Summers, who was a good friend of the Artisan Captain George Merrick, and his Vice-Captain Peter Roberts.

This action started a tradition that continues to the present. Indeed, in 1971 the club not only had the honour of entertaining the Irish Artisans for the first time, but also the pleasure of the company of John "Maurice" Jacobs. He had been friends with the Artisans both as a boy and a young man, and welcoming the famous golf teacher home was as good as honouring one of their own. As with Invitation Day, Captains Day developed other traditions. Perhaps the most famous of these was the establishment of the Halfway House, a convenient watering hole that was usually situated at the 13th tee. Manned for many years by Henry Knight it was, and still is, a welcoming sight on a hot day when the golf is not going to plan. Indeed, the story is told how Henry, who was "forced" to man it all afternoon, would be so drunk that he could hardly stand up by the end of the day!

The 1972 season was one for some amazing results. Jack Inman, who had been a member for over forty years, had never won a thing. In the space of three weeks he was to win four competitions, which included returning two 65's to win the Rose Bowl with lowest ever-recorded score! Michael Rowett, who had already won the Spencer Trophy, also won the Leng Cup, but was still able to card an eleven at the 16th in the process.

But 1973 saw the introduction of yet another new competition when Dennis Beaumont, who was the landlord of the Butchers Arms, acquired a trophy from Whitbread's brewery. Played as a bogey, it is still played for today.

Clive Betts, who had by this time established himself as the best player in the club, was invited to attend a trial for the Sheffield Union at Hillsborough Golf Club. Clive, who finished in the top twelve, never heard anymore. To this day it remains a mystery. His consistency continued, as he was the winner of the Denton Trophy for the best six medal rounds of the year in 1974.

1974 also saw the start of the Davenport Trophy, in memory of Neville Davenport who died suddenly on the course that year. Though he was not a member he was always keen to support the Artisans whenever he could.

1975 also saw some firsts as well. Like Jack Inman, Jack Lyon had been a member for over thirty years, and he too had never won a thing. This was to change when he won the Hallam Trophy, quite a feat when consideration is given to the fact that it comprised of one round of medal from the back tees to qualify, and then knockout to the final. In the same competition the following year, the final was contested by the brothers Jack and Oscar Clarkson, the first time this had happened in over forty years, when the winner was Oscar.

Towards the end of the decade a new name emerged. Ian Lilley, who was a green keeper on the course, found Lindrick very much to his liking. Armed with his graphite driver he was able to reduce many of the holes to just a drive and a short iron. With this advantage he won five competitions, which included the Leng Cup and the Rose Bowl, as well as the Denton Trophy and the Shireoaks Plate. For good measure he also took the new Horace Merrick Eclectic Trophy. It was a struggle for everyone else to keep up, but Ken Widdison rose to the challenge, by taking four titles that included the Kayser Cup, the Hallam Trophy, the Harrison Trophy, and the Spencer Trophy.

Though Ian continued to play he was not able to repeat his success again. Meanwhile 1979 saw the emergence of Alan Dexter as a serious player in the club. He too won five competitions, which included both the Leng Cup and Kayser Cup, but he also won the East Midlands Area Final of the Ford Competition with a net score of 70 playing off 14 handicap. The prize was a trip to Son Vida in Majorca to play in the national final. Though he had a great time, Alan was unable to land the ultimate prize.

Most of these successes were down to the individual skill of each player, but some of it was also down to the help of a man who had been at Lindrick for over fifty years. Jack Jacobs had come to Lindrick in 1924 when his uncle, Bob Jacobs, was appointed professional. From then until 1978 when he retired, Jack gave nothing but devoted service to Lindrick Golf Club, and his association with the Artisans was just as close. Indeed, he had been a honorary member since 1937, and repaid this kindness with impromptu golf lessons which normally took place on his route home along the 17th hole ,the practice ground and the 14th hole. As a result many an Artisan had reason to thank him for his help, which was always appreciated. In addition, credit was always available in his shop, and several Artisans, such as Ellis Colton and Jack Lyon, often caddied for him in the various professional tournaments which he played in. He was also a regular in team matches for the Artisans, though in 1971 George Robinson, the Artisan captain, sensationally dropped him! Nevertheless, his easy going manner made him universally popular not just at Lindrick, but also in the greater golfing world. Indeed, in 1969 he was awarded the prestigeous title of "Northern Club Professional of the Year".

Thus, at the end of the decade, as Jack Jacobs retired, a new era was about to begin, as the Artisans were about to face changes of their own, with redefined membership and playing conditions at the top of the list. Nevertheless, the club consisted of as many strong players as in the past, and although this position was to weaken over the next decade, the golfing strength was, for the moment, as good as ever.

CHAPTER 16
THE NORTHERN SECTION TOURNAMENT 1946-1998

Since the early 1920's, when J. H. Taylor helped form the Artisan Golf Association, the Artisans had always been involved in the tournaments held by the A. G. A. However, the problem with this was that it was largely a southern based organisation centred around the Home Counties. Not unnaturally this made communication between the clubs in the north and those in the south very difficult, and it was quite an involved process to play in any competitions. Thus, in 1928 a number of clubs in the north, including Lindrick, decided to form the northern section of the association. The result of this was that it was now easier to compete in competitions while it was also easier to organise the section.

The Artisans played almost every year but without any real success. It was not until after the war that the Artisans achieved the success that had been lacking. The breakthrough year was 1952 when the tournament was played at Lindrick for the first time. Played on Monday and Tuesday 16th and 17th June some fourteen players from the Artisans competed, including Jack and Wilf Hall, Jim Waterhouse, Jim Merrick, Colin Taylor, Roy Kipling, Ken

Northern Artisan Tournament 1952 at Lindrick. Len Salmon of Hoylake Village Players drives from the 13th tee watched by Len Riley of Buxton and High Peak and Roy Kipling of Woodsetts Artisans.
Owned by Roy Kipling.

Arnold Knowles and Jack Palmer at the Northern Tournament circa late 1950's.
Owned by Arnold Knowles.

Widdison and Bill Randall.

The tournament was played over 72 holes of medal, with the players divided in to two divisions based on handicap. The experience of playing at home was a big advantage to the Artisans, and the tight fairways and long rough caught many unprepared. Bill Randall, playing off four handicap shot 72,73 to lead the field by four strokes from Eric Ashmore of Buxton and High Peak.

This lead was to prove decisive as Bill shot 74,78 for a four round total of 297 to win the News Of the World Challenge Cup, presented to the golfer with the best 72 holes net, by one shot. Yet disaster nearly struck, as at the 15th Bill hit his second shot up against the wall, but was fortunate enough see it bounce back on to the green from where he was able to get his par. Eric Ashmore came second, but in third and fourth place were Ken Widdison and Colin Taylor on 303 and 304 respectively. In addition, Bill also won the Sir Lindsay Parkinson Rose Bowl which was competed for by players of eight handicap or better over 72 holes at this time. Overall, a very satisfactory tournament, and E. A. Barker, the Lindrick Captain and a future

Artisan President, then presented the trophies and prizes to the winners.

The net result of this stunning success was to fuel further interest, and success was not long in coming. The 1958 tournament was played at Buxton and High Peak, and it was here that the Artisans recorded their first "away" victory, when Colin Taylor won the News of the World Challenge Cup with scores of 70,74,70,67 for a four round total of 281 in some of the worst conditions in years. In-fact Colin won both the junior and senior sections and reduced his handicap from twelve to ten in the process. This was all the more remarkable because on the Sunday before the competition began, Colin set off at 10a.m from Lindrick with three other erstwhile members by the names of Doug Inman, Arnold Knowles and Doug Allen, but did not arrive in Buxton until 4.30p.m in the afternoon! It might be possible to believe that they had stopped off for some extra practice or that they stopped to talk tactics, but this would not be the case. In actual fact they had visited nearly every public house between Worksop and Buxton! Seemingly this steadied the nerves and victory was secured. In addition, the Artisans came second in the team competition five shots behind Buxton.

The early 1960's were very profitable years for the Artisans as success continued. The tournament was played again at Lindrick in 1961, and although they did not win the main prize this time, Jim Merrick won the Sir Lindsay Parkinson Rose Bowl for the best 36 holes net on the first day, as the tournament had been reduced from 72 to 54 holes and the nature of the trophies changed. Now, 36 holes were played by the seniors on the first day and 36 holes by the juniors on the second day, with prizes for 18 holes on the other day. Complicated as this may appear it had little effect on the Artisans, as the following year Roy Kipling won the trophy again- the first time the Rose Bowl had been retained by the club.

It was clear that the club was well motivated, and in 1964, at Maesdu Golf Club near Llandudno, Roy Kipling won The News of the World Challenge Cup. A few years later, probably in about 1968, the tournament was again played at Maesdu. Roy, although he did not win any of the main trophies that year was fortunate enough to win a senior prize. The excitement of winning was so great that Roy left part of his prize- a silver tray, at his apartment and it was only found when the rubbish was checked!

At Little Aston in 1965 George Robinson won the Sir Lindsay Parkinson Rose Bowl with scores of 74,72. The following year at Harrogate Golf Club, in perfect conditions- the best for some years, Bill Randall won the Rose Bowl to add to his 1952 triumph in the Challenge Cup with scores of 71,70 just pipping defending champion George Robinson! Also of significance was the play of Clive Betts who finished second in the News of the World Challenge Cup. Clive's first round 66 was the second best score of the week, and he only lost out on the main prize by virtue of finishing with a 73 to the eventual winner Joe Armitt's 69. Roy Kipling, writing in the Artisan Golfer some months later, said of this near miss, "Hard luck for Clive Betts, pipped on the post by Joe Armitt for the News of the World Trophy, but his turn must come, surely, and soon."

Though major success was not to come again until the 1970's, there was success for Vic Stocks in 1968 when the tournament was played at the Cavendish Golf Club in Buxton. Vic, playing off 18 handicap shot 73,68 to win the W.J. Gardner Cup- in memory of the former association secretary, for the best 36 holes in the junior division. It was a remarkable triumph, because not only was it the first time he had played in the tournament, it was also only two years since a serious back injury threatened to end his golf career.

Perhaps the most extraordinary story though was that recorded by Joe Mee in 1970. Joe, a member of the Artisans since the early 1920's, and a stalwart member since then, played in the junior division of the tournament held at Llandudno aged 66. In winning, Joe became the oldest ever champion, with scores of 68,72 and 76 to win by five clear shot's from the second placed player. In 1971, at Little Aston in the second week of June in very cold and cloudy conditions, that man George Robinson popped up again to win the News of the World Challenge Cup that had eluded him in 1965. With scores of 80, 69,78 for a total of 227 George beat T Gibson of Sutton Coldfield by two shots. In-fact, George's second round 69 was the best of the tournament in very difficult conditions on a tough course. Just for good measure, Oscar Clarkson won the Sir Lindsay Parkinson Rose Bowl with scores of 77,79.

The club was on a roll. By 1972 the potential of Clive Betts that had first shown itself in 1965 came good. The tournament was played at Grange Park Golf Club at St Helens in Lancashire. The weather was excellent with "glorious sunshine and blue sky's that were to last throughout the two days of the tournament", recalled Tom Burdell writing in the Artisan Golfer a few months later. The competition started at 8a.m when the Reverend Ramsden of Sutton Coldfield teed off with Sam Kendrick of Royal Birkdale and Clive Betts. Clive recalls how during the tournament much use was made of the local watering holes, but on the first day this did him no good at all as he shot an 81 gross in the scratch competition. Clearly requiring divine inspiration Clive rose to the challenge, and with steady nerves shot 74, 76 to win the Northern Championship Cup from T Gibson of Sutton Coldfield with a better last round. This trophy had been presented to the northern section by the late Western Cheshire Artisans Golf Club in 1964, which had been destroyed during the war. However, this was not good enough to win the News of the World Challenge Cup, as R Harper of Renishaw Park beat Clive by four shots.

In 1973 the tournament was held at Lindrick once more. However, things did not go as smoothly as in the past. Jack Clarkson, who was Chairman of the Association, and Tom Burdell, who was Secretary, argued about the allocation of places each club was entitled to. It was doubly difficult, as Jack was Secretary of Lindrick. Thus, there was a clash of interest, which soured the event. The committee commented:

"This was a bitter disappointment to several of our members who were regular competitors, and who had been unable to play because our entries had been cut by 50%".

To make matters worse the behaviour of some of the players left a lot to be desired, as it seemed many competitors were unaware of the basic etiquette of the game. Fortunately immediate action was taken and there has been no repeat performance since then.

Nevertheless, the competition got underway with great weather that lasted the whole tournament. The scoring was very moderate, which questioned the validity of the championship as the tournament was played from the front tees except for two holes where they were put forward. Clive Betts came second in the scratch competition, unable to retain his title that went to Alf Warwood of Sutton Coldfield, a winner on two previous occasions. Eric Taylor finished third on 242. However, the gloom was lifted when Len Morris, playing off eleven handicap, won the News of the World Cup with scores of 75,73,73 for a total of 221.

This represented something of a high point, as although both Roy Kipling and Doug Allen were to win the Sir Lindsay Parkinson Rose Bowl in 1975 at West Lancs. Golf Club with scores of 73,72, and 1976 at Maesdu Golf Club with scores of 70,69, the club was not to have any major success again until the late 1990's. Roger Merrick came second in the 1982 tournament played at Redcar, losing out by one shot, but by the mid 1980's the pilgrimage of players competing in the event had all but dried up. Only three players competed in 1984. Indeed, in 1989 the club had no players in either the senior or junior divisions, the first time since before the war. Only Colin Taylor represented the club when he played in, and won the Veterans section with 64 points, an event that Ken Widdison also won few years later.

What were the reasons for this dramatic decline? Perhaps the

Northern Tournament, Wallasey 1997. "New kids on the Block" David Rowett, Mark Merrick, Graham West and the experienced David Locke.
Owned by the author.

single biggest reason was that no young players were taking part in the tournament. When men such as Doug Allen, Roy Kipling, Colin Taylor, and George Robinson first started playing they were in the prime of their lives. The early 1980's heavily weighted the demography of the club to the senior members, and combined with the problems of down sizing the clubs' interest soon waned.

Perhaps though, a revival is at hand. By the early 1990's the club had reached its target membership of 60 members and was able to recruit new members on a one for one basis as in the past.

Graham West, Winner of the Harry Jackson and Frank Brookhose Trophy for the third division players at the Northern Tournament held at Cavandish Golf Club June 1998.
Owned by the author.

The net result of this was that a group of new members became interested in the tournament, who had no previous experience of the event. Thus in 1997, when the tournament was played at Wallasey on the Wirral, the Artisans sent ten competitors for the first time since 1983. True, the team consisted of some of the club stalwarts, such as Eric Taylor, Ken Widdison, David Locke, Terry Byrne and Alan Taylor, but it also had new blood in Ian Hunt, Roger Whitfield, Mark Merrick, Graham West, and David Rowett.

Indeed, this baptism was to be much valued, as in 1998 Graham West was to put the previous years experience to good use by winning the Harry Jackson Trophy for the best score in the recently formed third division. With a first round score of 36 points on the first day, Graham was well set up for the second day, when the event looked like not finishing when heavy rain threatened to spoil the day. In the end the third division was able to play nine holes, and Graham was fortunate enough to win this section of the competition as well with 20 points.

It is difficult to know whether this renaissance will be long lived, but while the health of the club remains strong, and new members find the event an attraction, it is likely that it will. Indeed, a winning member is always likely to encourage others to play, and perhaps after the success in 1998 this will be the case. The future then, remains open.

CHAPTER 17
UPSETTING THE APPLECART
1978-1980

In the late summer of 1977, a storm cloud appeared over the Artisans horizon, based on the rumour that Lindrick Golf Club wanted to reduce the size of the Artisan club membership. But as soon as the cloud appeared it seemed to disappear almost immediately. However, the next few years were to be toughest the Artisans had ever faced.

George Inman had been elected Captain at the A.G.M in 1977, and was enjoying his year of office like all previous captains before him, when in late July of 1978 he received a letter from Shaun Waide, the Lindrick Captain. Not suspecting anything he read the letter, and as it unfolded he knew things would never be the same again. It was a pivotal moment.

The contents of the letter were simple. The Artisans were to have their playing conditions redefined, based upon the assumption that inflation and rising costs were making it difficult "to maintain and develop Lindrick as a first class golf course of national repute". In short, new revenue had to be generated, and this could only be achieved by encouraging "visitors and societies" but "within the limitations necessary to avoid excessive wear and tear". Space could only be found to accommodate the increased number of visitors by restricting "the volume of play permitted by the members of the L.A.G.C". There was no mention of how many members the club could have, only that no new members should be admitted, and those existing members were entitled to play only two rounds of golf per week. Additionally, no play was to be allowed on Sunday mornings.

The shock wave that was generated by this announcement left the officials of the club in a state of deep trauma. While the world had changed around them the Artisans had carried on obliviously. But in truth the indications of change had been coming for some years, the problem was, of course, recognising it.

By the early 1960's golf had started to become a very popular sport, not only did new clubs emerge, but also television coverage brought the game to more people than ever before. This interest was fuelled by the emergence of the first golf superstars as players like Arnold Palmer, Jack Nicklaus and Gary Player brought style and razzmatazz to a game, that was still considered by many, to be one for old men.

Yet this was not all. A change in sporting interests was also matched by changes in social and demographic circumstances. Both Shireoaks and Woodsetts grew markedly in the 1960's, as new housing estates brought people in to the district who had no appreciation of their new environment, and Lindrick was no longer the quiet retreat it once was. Of course, the playing of the Ryder Cup in 1957 did not help that; neither did subsequent professional tournaments. Nevertheless the die had been cast.

At the same time the British economy was in decline, and by the 1970's inflation was wreaking havoc with businesses and individuals alike. In 1947 the Artisans paid an honorarium of 10 shillings to Lindrick Golf Club for the courtesy of the greens, by 1968 this had increased to £50. Ironically, the Artisans actually agreed to pay £70, and sent a cheque for that amount only to have £20 returned as it was considered to be too much! The committee commented that "this gesture of the Parent Club was very much appreciated, and expresses the goodwill that exists between the two club's".

Yet by September 1971 the situation had changed dramatically. Luke Seymour, the Lindrick Captain, had written to George Robinson, Captain of the Artisans, to discuss a more amicable arrangement regarding the annual honorarium to Lindrick Golf Club. A meeting was arranged for Friday 17th September to discuss the matter further, and a delegation comprising of George Robinson, Roy Kipling, Ellis Colton, and Jack Clarkson thrashed out the agreement over two hours of intense negotiations. With the support of a Vice President, Roy Summers, "very satisfactory arrangements... were made", which resulted in a 10% levy on every Artisan member based upon the annual full playing subscription of the Lindrick Golf Club. For the ladies this would be 5%. In essence, this increased the Artisans contribution to Lindrick Golf Club from £50 to £360.

This then was the background to the dramatic events of 1978:

events that were to stretch the relationship between the two clubs to virtual breaking point, a point that had never been reached before, and had never looked like coming near. Having recovered from the shock, the Artisans accepted the invitation of Shaun Waide to meet his Vice-Captain, Duncan McIntosh, and the Past Captain, David Craven, on Sunday August 13th to discuss the implementation of the proposals.

The fortnight between the receipt of the letter, and the date of the meeting were taken up discussing the strategy to be pursued. The Artisans main objections were that:

- There were to be no new members.
- Two rounds of golf per week were insufficient to facilitate competition and social play.
- Signing for rounds played was demeaning, and unworkable.
- There was no Sunday morning golf and other playing times were restrictive.
- Visitor's fees were unfair.
- Artisan play was excessive.

At this point only the officials of the club knew what was going on, and it was felt that it was best this way until after the meeting with Lindrick Golf Club. On the Sunday of the meeting the Artisan delegates were very nervous and apprehensive not knowing what to expect. Shaun Waide said from the outset "it was the desire of Lindrick Golf Club that the L.A.G.C should continue to enjoy the privileges of the course and past relationships with Lindrick Golf Club". George Inman was very relieved to hear this, and appreciated the "significant problems of maintaining a course of championship standard".

However, although this was all fine and well, it was also true to say that the Artisans would have preferred to have discussed the issues first rather than be presented with what looked like an ultimatum, as the deadline for implementation was 29th October 1978. The Artisan delegates raised their objections, but after two hours no significant progress had been made, other than an appreciation of where each side stood. The Lindrick delegates seemed surprised that the Artisan delegates could not make any decision without referring it to the general membership. At this point the meeting ended with the decision to meet again on August 27th to receive the answers to the proposals put to the Lindrick committee.

On Sunday August 27th the Artisan delegates once more met the representatives of Lindrick Golf Club to hear the responses to the requests they had made. Though cordial, the replies they received only partly met the aspirations of the Artisans. Sunday golf was to be allowed in winter, between 10.30 am and 11.30 am, but in summer early morning golf was banned. As membership was to be curtailed, Lindrick Golf Club agreed to give special dispensation for a member to resign so that his son or daughter could replace him, but this was to be a one off. Lindrick Golf Club also agreed that a "specially outstanding youngster" would be considered to play on the course so long as they were under parental control. They also indicated that they were looking for a total membership of about sixty, comprising of 48 men and 12 women. Finally, the numbers of rounds permitted per week was to stay at two, and the rounds were to be signed for in the professional's shop. The deadline for implementation was confirmed as 29th October 1978.

After the meeting Shaun Waide wrote back to George Inman with the revised proposals saying:

"My colleagues and I would like to express to you and your colleagues our thanks and admiration for the understanding and manner in which the discussions took place in what was bound to be a difficult problem for both of us...A Captains lot is not always a happy one."

At the next Artisan committee meeting on 9th September, careful consideration was given to the revised proposals, but on a majority decision they were rejected and the decision was made to seek legal advice. This was a decisive moment. The stakes had been raised, and what started out as friendly negotiations was now turning in to what looked like an industrial dispute: something that both sides did not want.

A letter was drafted and sent to the Secretary of Lindrick Golf Club stating the revised proposals were unacceptable, and that the implementation date be extended to 31st December. The Lindrick Captain was very disappointed with this decision, but it was too late to turn back. As the tension mounted a very sad event occurred when, by mutual consent, it was agreed to cancel the Artisans versus Lindrick match as, according to the Lindrick Secretary, it would be "less embarrassing for all concerned".

As winter came on there was still no likelihood of a decision being reached, but both sides continued to talk. On October 22nd an Extraordinary General Meeting was called to appraise the membership of what had happened and what the Committee was doing about it. The mood of the meeting was very sombre, and the Secretary commented that "there was scarcely a question from the members" highlighting the seriousness of the situation.

A further meeting with the Captain and officials of Lindrick Golf Club had taken place on 13th November, which though lasting over two and half-hours had achieved nothing. It was clear the proceedings were deadlocked. A fresh initiative was required, and this came from Jack Clarkson, who decided that the National Secretary, Tony Everett, might be able to help.

A meeting was arranged, and this, more than anything else kick-started the process again. The National Secretary was able to inform the Lindrick delegates more about the Artisan golfer at other clubs and told them that these members did quite a lot of light work on the course as part of the privilege of being extended the courtesy of the course. He went on to say that early Sunday morning golf was an accepted custom amongst other clubs, but controlled in a very disciplined manner. This took the Lindrick delegates by surprise, but it was important to the final outcome.

Nearly six months had elapsed since the first letter had passed between the two clubs, yet the two sides were still hardly any closer together. However, on December 7th the two sides met again and at last progress was made. The Artisans accepted that the membership had to be reduced, but sons of members should be given consideration even if this caused a temporary delay in the reduction of numbers, and that Lindrick employees were to be separate from the quota. In addition, Lindrick agreed to Sunday morning golf- but in a revised format- that was based around foursomes and singles play. Players had to be off the first tee by 8.00am and past the 8th hole by 9.30am.

In return for these concessions the Artisans agreed to undertake light work on the course when required, and also bunker raking duties during the summer months. The problem of security on the course, which had tendered to worsen in previous years, was to be tackled by having two Artisans patrol the course on Saturday and Sunday between 8.00am and 8.00pm.

However, although this moved the two sides closer together, the major sticking point of how many rounds could be played per week was still at issue. The Artisans felt that a high price was being paid for the concessions Lindrick had agreed, and the decisive factor in the general membership accepting the revised conditions may come down to whether they could play three rounds per week instead of two. The Lindrick officials responded by saying that as the membership declined this point could be reviewed on an annual basis. Though less than satisfactory, the Artisans said they would take the revised terms back to the general committee for consideration at the next meeting in early January 1979.

The winter of 1979 was quite bad, and the country was suffering the worst industrial disputes for some years. The infamous "winter of discontent" was having an effect on everyone, and it was in this background that the committee arranged for a special A.G.M to be held on Sunday 29th January to discuss the proposals with the membership.

Some 53 members attended the meeting, but after a long debate rejected the new proposals. The main problem areas were the number of rounds that could be played each week, as well as the question of patrolling the course on weekends for security reasons. On the one hand, it was felt that two rounds was insufficient to meet all playing needs, while on the other, the issue of security was putting the members at unacceptable risk. The meeting did not give, however, any clear indication to the Artisan delegates as to which direction to go next, only that no agreement should be reached "without the approval of the membership in a general meeting".

Time though was pressing on, and an agreement needed to be reached before the start of the new season, which was rapidly approaching. Lindrick were very disappointed with the outcome, but a change in personnel at the end of January brought a different response to what may have been expected. At the Lindrick Golf Club A.G.M, the new Captain, Duncan McIntosh, decided to force the issue to a conclusion. In what could only be described as bit of a surprise, the Lindrick committee agreed to allow the Artisans three rounds per week, and adjust the security element to an informal, rather than a formal one.

Thus, on 11th February 1979, some six months on from the original communication, the general membership of the Artisan club accepted the revised conditions. Effectively, it meant the argument was over. Things would never be like before, but in the following years, fourball matches would return on Sunday mornings, starting times would be reviewed, and the total membership would be established at sixty. The result of this was that during the early 1990's new members were being accepted as in the past, something that seemed very unlikely in 1979.

In the end common sense prevailed, and this moment of madness only served to realign the relationship between the two clubs', while those forces that were hell bent on pulling them apart were shocked at the speed at which old associations re-established themselves. Today, the relationship between the clubs is better than ever, and the twice-annual fixture, which at one point looked destined for the scrap heap, flourishes healthily allowing old friendships to continue and new ones to begin. ·

CHAPTER 18
THE IRISH QUESTION 1970-1999

At the end of the 1960's, as the political situation in Northern Ireland was starting to deteriorate, golfing relations with the Republic of Ireland were just about to begin. The Artisans were the ambassadors of the this process, a process that to this day remains as strong as it was thirty years ago, as in late spring the Irish Artisans make their annual pilgrimage to the hallowed turf at Lindrick.

In June 1970 the Northern Section Tournament was held at Maesdu Golf Club near Llandudno. Several members attended the event and they included Doug Allen, Len Morris, and Colin Taylor. They had decided to make a holiday of the week, and had read in the Artisan Golfer an article from the Irish Artisans wanting to establish an international match with the National Association of England. Doug Allen, who was always keen to meet new people and see new places in the pursuit of his favourite past time, had written beforehand explaining how the Lindrick Artisans were keen establish a

Captains Day 1991. Peter Archbold, Jack McGeer, Keith Spencer, Tom Kinch, and Joe Rylands.
Owned by Mick and Iris Hall.

match. After the tournament, the intrepid explorers set off for the ferry at Holyhead, and once in Dublin made their way to Woodbrook Golf Club where the Carrolls Irish Tournament was being played.

There, Jack McGeer, Treasurer of the Irish Artisan Association, the President, Michael Carroll, the Honorary Secretary, Pat Kenny, and the Captain, Michael Sinnot, welcomed them. Co-opted as stewards, they were put in the same hotel as the tournament's organisers, and treated like royal guests. All of this was completely unexpected and the Artisans saw it as a great honour. The meeting was so successful that an invitation was extended to the Irish Association to attend the Artisans Captains Day in June 1971 at Lindrick. Mission accomplished; and many a Guinness later, the gallant band returned triumphantly home.

Though know one at the time realised it, this was a formative moment, not just for the Artisans of Lindrick, but also for the whole of the Artisan movement, as a new chapter was to begin in Anglo-Irish relations. All of this was in counterpoise to the terrible events that were happening in Ulster.

Thus, in early June 1971 the Irish Artisans came to play at Lindrick in George Robinson's Captain's Day. Five Irish association members attended, including Jack McGeer and Pat Kenny. They all had a wonderful time, some staying with the families of Artisan members. Pat Kenny summarised the feelings of them all when he said:

"Having been one of the lucky five to play in [Captain's day], I find it hard indeed to express in words, on behalf of my friends and associates our thanks for the wonderful reception we received on and off the course. It was a special pleasure to meet...all those wonderful Artisans and lady associates at Lindrick."

Although the golf was the main concern, there was also business to be attended to as well. At this time the Irish were joined by Bill Farley, Secretary of the A.G.A, and John Hooker, Recording Secretary, to discuss the possibility of an international match between the two associations. Bill Farley was adamant about this when he said, "an international match against Ireland can, and must, be the result."

They were not to be disappointed. The Artisans made several visits to the Irish association, but it was not until September 1975 that the first international match took place at Walton Heath, when the Irish won a close match by eight matches to six. This match continues to this day, and from time to time the Artisans have sent players to compete in this prestigious event.

In 1978, for example, the match was played in Dublin when thirty-one players from twelve English clubs attended. The teams consisted of twenty a side, though where the other eleven went is uncertain, and the match was played at Grange Golf Club just outside Dublin. Again the English Artisans were given a lesson, as 17 matches were heavily lost, with only 3 wins in reply! Why this was such a crushing defeat is uncertain, but Doug Allen, writing in the Artisan Golfer sometime after the match, was able to offer a partial explanation when he said they were served whiskey and Guinness for breakfast every morning! Though clearly ambushed, Doug continued by saying that the important thing was that:

"The main theme of the weekend was that the results of the match were not too important- it's the bond that is being forged between us that counts."

The match continued to enjoy popularity, but by 1981, when the match was played at Clontarf Golf Club, interest was starting to decline. Where previously twenty or thirty players had attended it was now down to less than ten. The match was again lost 6 1/2 to 2 1/2, with both Doug Allen and Colin Taylor losing 4 and 3. Only George Robinson from the Artisans managed to get anything from the match as he halved his game with M. McLouhlin. An uncharacteristically downbeat Doug Allen wrote:

"We were no match for our opponents and were convincingly beaten. Our biggest disappointment was not that of losing the match, but not have having provided sterner opposition...I appreciate the difficulties that arise in getting   enough low handicap golfers for the away match...[but]...a fresh look must be given to this most enjoyable get together."

Though the international match seemed to be having problems, the original group kept coming to Lindrick on subsequent Captains Days. From time to time the personnel changed, but ever constant was Jack McGeer. He built up a very strong friendship with all the Artisans, but in particular Colin Taylor, who gave him lodgings and hospitality that was second to none. In fact things were so organised that Colin's mother provided the accommodation for the others, giving them a free run of her house!

By the mid 1980's there was a change, as a fresh group of men came to Lindrick. Jack was still ever present, but Joe Rylands, Tom Kinch, and Peter Archbold, who were all members of Elm Park along with Jack, now accompanied him. This group remained largely unchanged until 1992 when Jack McGeer died. The previous year he had been presented with a rose bowl to commemorate twenty years of coming to Lindrick.

Jack McGeer, though one of the most gracious and affable of men, was also a wily old campaigner, who played golf to win. He very rarely lost, and when he did it was considered to be of almost national importance! Mick Hall played with Jack on many occasions and invariably came back out of pocket. However, at Elm Park in 1990 Mick managed to win a £5 off him. The event was so significant that

Captains Day 1991. Jack McGeer receives a silver rose bowl to mark his 20th anniversary of visiting Lindrick. Colin Taylor, Arnold Knowles, Mick and Iris Hall are in attendance.
Owned by Mick and Iris Hall.

Mick got Jack to sign and date it as proof forever of the event. Today the note resides in its own display case with a photograph of Jack, at Mick's home.

In the main the Irish Artisans have found it difficult to play successfully at Lindrick, and have tried many different routines to find the winning formulae. Entitled to the courtesy of the course on the Sunday evening before Captains Day, for which thanks are extended to Lindrick Golf Club, they have tried playing once, twice, and even not at all- but all to no avail!

According to Tom Kinch and Peter Archbold, it no longer matters. The important point is that every year they get invited, and every year they look forward to visiting Lindrick, meeting up with their old friends and also making new ones. In many ways it has become as much a social event, as a golfing one. Joe Rylands introduced some members to a particular Irish beverage known as Poteen; an illicit alcoholic drink made from potatoes. The Artisans prided themselves on being able to hold their own with anyone, but in this instance the Irish won, as one member, when hitting the air outside the clubhouse, allegedly fell over! In-fact, nights after matches often became blended with days, and on one occasion the 18th hole was played at 6.30am, but without any success, or any reason.

Whilst the Irish have been entertained at Lindrick, so the Artisans have been in Ireland. In the early days Doug Allen, Colin Taylor and George Robinson were the Artisan representatives, but by the mid 1980's a new group took up the pilgrimage to the Emerald Isle.

In 1989 Mick and Iris Hall, along with Keith and Sylvia Spencer, visited Ireland for the first time. The trip was planned for August as this coincided with the annual Irish Artisan Golf Festival. It was also an opportunity to have a holiday as well, thus killing two birds with the proverbial one stone.

It was a very successful trip, as Keith won a second prize in the Nines competition with Keith Archbold, the son of Peter, at Bray. At the end of their trip around Ireland the intrepid bunch had been recording their adventures to the tune of the song the "Wild Rover". At the end of the trip they met up with the Irish Artisans again to sing their story. It was received to tumultuous applause, and was so successful that they were forced to do an encore!

In 1990 they went again, where they were the guests of Jack McGeer and his wife Jesse. To their great surprise they were given the courtesy of Elm Park Golf Course, which was where Jack McGeer was a member. As usual the hospitality extended was beyond expectation, and a great time was had by all.

The Irish Artisans always had a good relationship with the lady members at Lindrick, and in 1988 they extended their invitation to the ladies to come over to Ireland and play them in a match before Captains Day. The challenge was duly accepted, and the ladies team consisted of Iris Hall, Bessie Brewer, Lorraine Hall and Alice Morris. Both Lorraine and Alice had never been out of the country before and were understandably nervous, but once the ferry had left Holyhead they too were up for the match. As usual Jack McGeer, who introduced them to Irish hospitality before the game, was at the dockside to welcome them. In the match they played with Jack, Peter Archbold, Joe Rylands, and Tom Kinch. The game was so successful that they went again in 1989.

Since then other Artisans have visited the Irish Association, such as Terry Byrne and Richard Tweed, while in 1997 a welcome return was made by Colin Taylor after some years due to illness and injury.

Ireland 1988. Bessie Brewer and Alice Morris at Elm Park.
Owned by Bessie Brewer.

Though their relationship with Lindrick goes back slightly less than thirty years, it has been so significant that it is difficult to imagine what it would have been like without it. Thirty years ago, as trouble flared in Northern Ireland, the Artisan golfers of England and the Republic, saw fit to start something new. How ironic then, that as peace returns to the north of Ireland that the relationship between the Irish and the Artisans remain as strong as ever.

CHAPTER 19
LINDRICK ON THE BIG STAGE
1957-1988

Since the first ball had been struck at Lindrick in 1891, the club had held its fair share of important tournaments, though mostly these were fairly modest affairs such as the Sheffield Open or the Yorkshire Amateur Championship. In the 1950's this was to change dramatically as Lindrick was propelled on to the big stage with a vengeance.

Why it took Lindrick so long to stage a major professional tournament is not exactly certain, as the course had been regarded as a stern test of golf for many years. Perhaps the missing ingredient was desire, and the will of one person, or group of people to make it happen. From the 1950's this combination all came together at once, and the Artisans were to play an important role in the success of the tournaments that followed.

Sir Stuart Goodwin, who was a Sheffield businessman, had been a Lindrick member since 1936, and it had long been his desire to stage a major professional tournament at Lindrick. This looked likely in 1939, but the outbreak of war caused this to be abandoned to everyone's disappointment. With this in mind he approached the P. G. A to hold his own tournament at Abbeydale in 1952. It was so successful that the tournament was played at Lindrick in September 1953, with the intention of holding a major tournament some time later. The contribution of the Artisans was quite modest, but the lady members were asked to assist with catering for the Lindrick members and the caddies of the tournament. The job must have been done well as a letter was received from Sir Stuart "thanking the Artisans for their services during the Goodwin tournament".

At this time the P. G. A was in financial difficulties and was looking to find a venue for the 1957 Ryder Cup matches. Seeing an opportunity, Goodwin offered a large donation to the P. G. A to play the match in the Sheffield area. In the end only Lindrick was considered suitable, a fact which Sir Stuart knew perfectly well. In many ways this caused some consternation amongst many golf commentators, who feverishly thumbed through their road atlases to locate Lindrick's position. By March 1956 the matter was settled, and the Artisans committee agreed:

"That congratulations be sent to Lindrick Golf Club for the honour of being selected to [host] the Ryder Cup in 1957, and to state that the Artisan club will be prepared to give all the assistance possible."

Lindrick Golf Club fully appreciated the offer and by early 1957 plans were finalised. The club agreed to marshall one hole and requested the 1st or the 18th holes, but in the end the club was allocated the 2nd hole. In addition, the clubhouse was to be used by the St Johns Ambulance Brigade as a base for their first aid operations.

By July the excitement was increasing as the drill for stewarding was received. George Dinsdale was chosen as team leader, and was ably assisted by Frank Stothard. The Artisans also contributed in other ways too. As the start came ever closer they helped stake out the course. George Dinsdale and Jack Clarkson, along with Jack Palmer, the butcher from Shireoaks, volunteered for this task, while Roy Kipling, for instance, offered to undertake scoreboard duties.

Finally, as the tournament started caddies were required for the teams. At a time when

Fred Hawkins with caddy Colin Taylor, Ryder Cup 1957.
Owned by Colin Taylor.

the professional caddy was still a long way off, those who knew the course best came forward to show the way. In the main it was the American team who required the help, as the majority of the British and Irish team brought their own caddies. George Merrick had the bag of Briton Peter Mills, while the bags of Americans Ed Furgol, Fred Hawkins, Tommy "Thunder" Bolt, Ted Kroll, Doug Ford, Jack Burke and Dick Mayer were carried by Len Morris, Colin Taylor, Ellis Colton, Eric Taylor, Bill Randall, Jim Merrick and Doug Inman.

The result of the match was an emphatic British and Irish victory by 7 1/2 to 4 1/2, but the caddies believed the Americans were slightly blasé as they enjoyed a good time in Nottingham. Colin Taylor, who caddied for the American Fred Hawkins, said he had never met a more generous man and was humbled by his graciousness in defeat- a defeat that had been twenty-four years in the waiting. From the start of the second day when the Americans were winning comfortably, there was a change in the atmosphere that grew amongst the crowd and the home players.

Unused to these type of events the crowds turned out in their thousands to cheer on Dai Rees' team. Tommy Bolt, whose caddy was Ellis Colton, started to feel the pressure as the drama unfolded, and not renowned for his patience, began to lose his control. Ellis recalls, how on that fateful Saturday, Bolt cracked under the strain. In the morning round against Eric Brown, (the singles were played over 36 holes at this time) they arrived at the 18th hole. The wind was from behind and Ellis suggested a 4 iron, but Bolt's shot was poorly executed and finished short of the green. In a raging temper Bolt turned to Ellis and said "You f****** live around here, and you don't know which way the f****** winds blowing!" More was to come.

In the afternoon Bolt hit a poor shot at the short 6th and proceeded to bury his club in to the tee. At the 15th Brown had won by 4 and 3, but not after more antics that included a broken club, more bad language, and arguments with E. A. Barker, the referee. Roy Kipling, writing in the Artisan Golfer some years later, was the scoreboard carrier in this match and remembers these extraordinary scenes with amazement.

"Bolt would have been banished to the clubhouse around the 14th ...Bad language, arguing with the referee, throwing golf clubs -the lot.

Small wonder the Indians, as he described the [crowd] were unfriendly...It was a golfing memory I will never forget!"

Lindrick had arrived, and the Artisans had performed their duties without reproach. Letters of thanks were received from the captain of Lindrick Golf Club and W. A. Gardner, Honorary Secretary of the Artisan Golfers Association, thanking the club for all their efforts.

Three years later, in 1960, Lindrick once again played host to a major international golf event, when this time it was the turn of the amateur ladies to take on the Americans in the Curtis Cup. Could lightning strike twice in the same spot? Actually no, as the Americans ran out easy winners by 2 1/2 to 6 1/2. Nevertheless, the Artisans volunteered to assist with stewarding and roping and several members caddied for the triumphant Americans. Indeed, one of the Americans playing that week was the little known Joanne Gunderson,

American Curtis Cup team 1960. Caddies left to right Jim Merrick, Eric Taylor, Johnny Hall (non Artisan), Colin Taylor, Bill Randall, Jack Shepherd (non Artisan), and Alan Ibberson (non Artisan).
Owned by Eric Taylor.

who over the next twenty-five years was to be better known as the professional Joanne Carnner.

By now Lindrick had well and truly caught the tournament bug, and in 1966 the first 72 hole professional competition was played at Lindrick when the Dunlop Company played their masters tournament. Once more the Artisans were asked to assist and once more they rose to the challenge. Caddying was under-taken by one or two members, and Colin Taylor caddied for Jock Panton of Scotland. Help was required with stewarding, roping, lunch boxes, and car parking. One unusual request though was for a local information officer. This had come directly from Dunlop's publicity department, who had written to the Worksop Town Council asking for advice on who would be the best person for the job. The council advised Dunlop's to write to the Artisans to see if they could assist. Strangely enough, Jack Clarkson, who worked for the council, accepted the job, and he was to be found in the information booth situated in the tented village located behind the clubhouse in Sir Wilton-Lee's field!

Only forty invited competitors took part in the tournament, which included Peter Thomson, Bob Charles, Roberto de Vicenzo, Tony Jacklin, Peter Allis, and the eventual winner Neil Coles. The tournament also included some lesser-known players such as Hugh Boyle of Ireland, who was playing out of the John "Maurice" Jacobs Golf School. At the second hole, which the Artisans had once again been allocated to steward, Boyle put his ball in to the rough. When Boyle got to his ball he accused George Dinsdale, who was the chief steward for the hole, of standing on it. For anyone who knew George this was a serious accusation to make, and a big mistake! After dressing Boyle down, in a manner in which the language was "blunt and to the point", according to Trevor Dinsdale, Boyle proceeded to play the ball from its original resting-place. Hitting the ball cleanly it finished in the middle of the green. Boyle then turned to George and said, "Come and stand on my ball again!"

The P. G. A returned to Lindrick once more in 1975 when the Sun Alliance Match Play Championship was staged. At the time this was the oldest P. G. A event dating back to the turn of the century when James Braid won the title. Unlike previous tournaments Lindrick Golf Club did not ask the Artisans to steward any particular hole, but asked for volunteers to fill many different roles. The Chief steward, Dougal Rae, who was to be an Artisan President in years to come, co-ordinated the various teams with great aplomb, which included all the usual activities. After the event he wanted to learn as much as possible about how this had gone, and invited the Artisans to give feedback on the various points that could be utilised for future events.

This was not long in coming, as in 1977 the Ladies Open Championship was being played for the first time. This event was played in late August, and was a great success. 1977 was to be a busy year as the Dunlop Masters returned to Lindrick for the second time. Once more the Artisans performed various duties that included roping, stewarding, board carrying, car parking, and caddying. In-fact, Colin Taylor caddied for Hubert Green, the then holder of the U. S Open Championship in the practice rounds, while Roy Rowett and Ken Widdison assisted with the staking of the course. The Artisan Captain, Brian Dinsdale, was invited along with his wife Sheila to the V. I. P Dinner that that preceded the championship, a new feature that was coming in to corporate sponsored golf at this time.

The tournament itself was played in some very wet and windy conditions, with the result that the course record was never likely to be beaten. In the end Guy Hunt beat Brian Barnes after a play off that lasted three holes.

The early 1980's saw the Martini International tournament played in 1982, remembered more for Greg Norman's 14 at the 17th, than for Bernard Gallacher's seven under par winning score. Again various duties were performed, but by now corporate sponsored events were being organised increasingly through contract work. As in 1977 the tournament was preceded by a pro-am, in which Norman Tyson was lucky enough to play with Brian Waites, the Ryder Cup Golfer, by virtue of winning a special competition. In addition, the Captain, Doug Allen was also invited to play.

During the 1980's Lindrick was used as the regional qualification course for the Open Championship for several years. Ball spotters and other volunteers were required. Again the Artisans came forward to assist. In 1988 the course held its last major professional tournament when the ladies European tour returned with the Weetabix

Ladies Open championship. Again, the Artisans performed various duties with distinction, which included caddying and car parking.

In a high quality field, that included Alison Nicholas- local girl and reigning champion, U. S Open champion Laura Davies, and several top American and Australian players; Corrine Dibnah of Australia came through the field to win the title. Of interest was the fact that George Hutchinson, who was a St Johns Ambulance volunteer, had to attend to a spectator who had been hit with a ball that had been struck by the winner. Also from a caddying point of view, veteran member George Merrick, caddied for Kathy Imrie, the leading amateur, while Ken Widdison shouldered the bag of the American Wendy Wisburn. Both looked resplendent in their yellow boiler suits!

1982 Martini International. Norman Tyson partners Ryder Cup player Brian Waites in the Pro-Am.

Owned by Lindrick Artisans Golf Club.

By the end of the 1980's the tournament scene had just about run its course. It was becoming increasingly difficult to accommodate spectators and players in an area where hotel accommodation was somewhat limited. In addition, the A57 trunk road had become much busier in the 1980's as more freight was transported by road than rail. This made it quite a major operation to control the traffic at the 12th and 17th holes. No longer was it possible to close the road as had been done in 1957, and business was increasingly impatient to receive its goods on time. Yet one last hurrah was possible in 1991, when the amateur golfers of England and Spain played an international match. Assistance was required again, which was, as ever, forthcoming. Ken

Widdison caddied for the Spaniard Elvaro Pratt who lost to Jim Payne who later turned professional.

Whether any more professional tournaments will be played at Lindrick is uncertain. However, what can be said with certainty is that the Artisans will always be there to offer assistance when required, and Lindrick Golf Club have always been grateful for this help.

CHAPTER 20
THE RISE AND FALL OF THE LADIES 1946-1998

The twenty ladies were an integral part of the Artisans: even though they had their own organisation, their own competitions, and were also members of the Ladies Golf Union. But their story in the second half of the century is one of great achievement and equally one of great decline.

To begin to understand this, something needs to be known about who the ladies were. In the immediate post-war period the lady members were largely those of the pre-war years. Vivian Jacobs, Kitty Spencer, Edith Bowles, and Janet Twibell formed the core, but there were some recent additions in Alice Morris, Jessie Rowett and Bessie Brewer. This small group of women were to enjoy the next thirty years, not just from a golfing point of view, but also from a social point of view as the two sides of the club enjoyed a particularly special relationship.

It is quite easy to see how this came about. The majority of the women were married to men who were also members. For example, Jessie Rowett was married to Roy Rowett, Alice Morris was married to Len Morris, and Joan Widdison was married to Ken Widdison to name just a few. In addition, they all lived close together in either Woodsetts or Shireoaks, and their daily lives invariably crossed. These were literally the days when there was no need to lock your doors, and everyone in the villages knew each other. They were then, by one means or another, all very close with one another.

Indeed, the relationship with the men was one of a partnership, where the role of the women was in support of the men. For example, they would be expected to support the men at various official engagements, such as preparing the meals after team matches, as in 1954 when the Artisans from Ogden (Halifax) were entertained, while six ladies volunteered to help prepare teas for the caddies in the 1949 Yorkshire Amateur Championship. From time to time they were also involved in cleaning the clubhouse, which also included sharing the cost of maintaining and improving the clubhouse. In 1947, for example the ladies gave £5 towards the installation of running water and toilet facilities, while in 1965 the ladies had their own locker room installed for the sum of £4, and four additional lockers built at a cost of £3/11/10d. The ladies contributed £1 towards these improvements!

From an organisational standpoint Janet Twibell was Honorary Secretary from the early 1920's until her retirement in 1960, when she was well into her 80's. She was held in great esteem, and Jack Clarkson was a great admirer, while in the 1960's and 1970's Lily Inman held the position. She too was well respected, and was very meticulous in the running of the club. In 1971, when Iris Hall joined, she saw Lily as someone to be looked up to. Indeed, "she was to the ladies, what Jack Clarkson was to the men". Other members have held this post including Gwen Swift, and Joan Ashurst, while since 1990 Iris Hall has held the position.

From a golfing point of view team matches were played as before. Worksop ladies were popular opponents, but proved very difficult to beat. On May Day 1950 the Artisans lost at home by 7 1/2 to 1 1/2, the halves being gained by Mrs Taylor, Mrs Twibell, and Mrs Inman. In September of that year they lost the return 5 1/2 to 3 1/2, while in May 1951 total disaster struck when they lost by 7 to 0. Still, better luck was had against the Lindrick ladies when they drew four games all in October 1950. Mrs Steadman, Mrs Bowles, Mrs Goacher, and Mrs Waterhouse all secured victories in the tie. In 1954 the ladies beat Lindrick by 4 1/2 to 3 1/2, but again lost to Worksop by 4 matches to 3. Yet in 1958 the ladies got their revenge when they heavily defeated their nemesis 7 1/2 to 1/2 at Lindrick.

Competitive though they were, winning and lowering their handicaps was not the over-riding priority until the late 1960's. At this time a lady by the name of Mary Ingham joined the club. She was not born and bred in the villages, and had a different outlook on the game that the members were not used to. She was strong and powerful and could play to 18 handicap or less, which made things very hard for the other members. The result was that the core members suddenly had to start to play better, with the consequence that they became more competitive. Club competitions still took part for the Lady Bingham

Trophy, and Carr Rose Bowl, but there was also the addition of the Spencer Trophy in 1968 for added spice. In addition the ladies also had their own Captains Day and Invitation Day, and these were just as popular as those of the men's section. The prizes though were very interesting. Often they would be odd silver spoons, trays, and garden fork and trowel sets! Nevertheless, the club prospered, and soon it was to pay off in a big way.

Lindrick Ladies Artisans Golf Club 1972. Top left to right Muriel Maloney, Jessie Rowett, Bessie Brewer, Alice Morris, Josie Taylor, Lily Inman, Edith Bowles, Majorie Allen, Ivy Betts. Bottom left to right Kitty Spencer, Nancy Merrick, Joan Widdison, Gwen Swift, Stephanie Betts, Olive Dinsdale, Ruth Leadale, Majorie Merrick, Betty Allen, and Gwen Steadman.
Owned by Bessie Brewer.

In September 1975 four of the ladies, who included Iris Hall, Bessie Brewer, Alice Morris, and Jessie Rowett competed at Garforth for the Ladies Inter-Club Team Trophy. There were some forty other teams taking part, so it was a great surprise when the team won with a score of 306- some ten shots better than the next nearest team! More was to come. Alice Morris won the best individual prize, a glass and silver claret jug, with a net score of 69. Iris, who had borrowed her husband's car to convey the team, then led the victorious group in song back down the M1 to Lindrick. By the time they arrived a group of members were there to meet them, including some of the husbands. The rest of the night was then spent celebrating in style, with the singing of more songs and drinking from the cup. Having achieved a great team success they returned in 1976 to retain the title. Again they won by a clear margin, and this time Jessie Rowett won the best individual prize, while each team member won a silver place mat. But could they have achieved the hat trick? Unfortunately we will never know, as the following year their application to compete was rejected. No real reason was given, and they were asked to bring the trophy back as soon as possible. Not surprisingly this left a bitter taste of disappointment in the mouth that for a time was hard to swallow.

Ladies Inter Club Competition, Garforth 1975. The lady Captain Kitty Spencer congratulates Alice Morris, winner of the individual prize, while team members Bessie Brewer, Jessie Rowett, and Iris Hall look on.

Owned by Jessie Rowett.

Why had they been so successful? It is difficult to know precisely, but Iris Hall believed it was due to two reasons. Firstly, Lindrick was a hard course, which demanded accuracy and patience, Garforth, though not an easy course was a little less demanding. Secondly, the ladies who competed were used to this type of competition, as they often played in inter-club mixed competitions at other courses. Additionally, they were experienced players, and at this time they were at the peak of their game. Yet, this victory represented the high point for the ladies, because the average age of the members was well over fifty, and although there were some younger members coming through, there were not enough new ones to fill the void that was starting to build at the back.

Though the Garforth victories represented the pinnacle achievement of the club, perhaps some of their best times were when the ladies played with the men in mixed competitions, both at home and away. In 1949 a mixed greensome was played, and although the result is not known Jack Clarkson was able to say:

"It has engendered great enthusiasm in the ladies section, and has created a real sporting team spirit among all members."

Mixed foursomes competitions continued for many years, but during the 1950's they were very popular. In 1953 for instance Gwen Steadman and Bill Randall won the competition played on August 14th by 1/2 a shot from Eva Waterhouse and George Merrick who shot a net 72, while Jim Waterhouse and Bessie Brewer came third. Often these matches were organised by the club Captains and in 1957 Edith Bowles and Jack Hall organised the competeition, which was won by Bessie Brewer and Ken Widdison who shot a net 65.

Indeed, many away matches were played at local clubs. The early 1960's were famous for trips to Elsham in north Lincolnshire. These outings attracted many competitors and the Artisans were always well represented, when upwards of twenty or so members would attend. Mick and Iris Hall came second at Elsham instead of Doug Allen and Bessie Brewer because they forgot to sign their card. Doug, who was a stickler for the rules, was, for once, speechless! Though winning was important, it was far from the be-all and end-all, as it was as much a social event as a golfing one. Many a long night was spent at the Red Lion at Redbourne on the way home; and fond reminiscing took place for several days afterwards. But it was all good clean fun though, enjoyed by a very close knit group of friends, whose raison d'être was to have a good time. Tankersley was also a famous haunt for the Artisans, and often the story is told of how Doug Allen and Bessie Brewer got lost on the way to the course. Taking a wrong turn they found themselves on the 18th hole heading towards the clubhouse. Other member's, who had arrived early, suddenly saw the car and realised whose it was, while golfers from other clubs wondered what was going on!

Artisans at Elsham circa early 1960's.
Owned by Bessie Brewer.

Success in these matches was had from time to time. In 1972, at the 50th anniversary of Rushcliffe, Ken and Joan Widdison won first prize in the mixed section with a net 66 1/2. The following year, again at Rushcliffe, George and Nancy Merrick won with a net 64 from Roy and Jesse Rowett whose score of 69 1/2 was not quite enough. Meanwhile, in the same year Eric Taylor and his aunt, Lily Inman, won an open meeting at Coxmoor. But all of this was about to change.

The re-negotiation of playing conditions in 1978 became the catalyst for a decline that in 1998 had still not bottomed out. From a high of twenty members in 1978 there was a slow and gradual deterioration over the next decade as the older members literally became unable to play. However, there was one significant difference to this general pattern. In 1979 a new member joined by the name of Lorraine Hall. She was to marry and be better known as Mrs Thorlby, and over the next twelve years or so was to dominate the ladies game of the club. She did not have everything her own way however as Iris Hall, no relation, Alice Morris, Joan Widdison, and Bessie Brewer ensured that it was not all one way traffic.

By the late 1980's the club was approaching crisis point however. Membership was dwindling, (there were only eleven members in 1989) and those new members who came in as replacements were not as interested as first seemed. The issue was not just one of numbers, but more importantly the right numbers. The new rules governing membership in 1978 meant that for the first few years only the daughters of members were eligible, and even when this was changed to relatives of members in the mid 1980's there was little or no improvement. There was some sympathy with the ladies on the matter, but when it was agreed the total membership must be 60, the problem then became one of determining the male-female split. In December 1989, Joan Ashurst (the ladies secretary) argued that the figure should be 15, pointing out that they should receive " a new member on alternative years to the men's section, depending on availability of vacancies". The men's Committee was forced to accept that the present situation was undesirable, and the ladies "section was almost not viable, but under the present ruling non-relatives cannot be considered". To help ease the situation the men's committee agreed in 1987 that the lady captain and vice-captain could attend the men's meeting when vacancies were being discussed, but that the final decision on membership would rest with the men. This was accepted.

But trouble was lurking. For some reason in 1988 the ladies were not invited to the men's committee meeting. This caused such great upset in the ladies section that they unilaterally decided to manage their own affairs, and offered membership to an applicant without submitting it to the men's committee. In response to the situation the committee despatched the Captain and Secretary to discuss the issue. Fortunately the situation was soon resolved, and the committee agreed to accept the new member.

Though communication was the issue, the position did not improve overnight, and it was not until 1991, when it was decided that the ladies should be invited to attend two meetings per year, "to discuss matters pertaining to both sections prior to the main meeting" that something was done. Relief was at hand, when the Parent Club in the same year agreed that membership was not confined to close family relations, but anyone who resided in the qualifying area and who were not members of other club's. Ironically, this was a return to the agreement of 1964 where prospective members were required to live in the qualifying area. The outline of the agreement was that the club should be composed of 46 male and 14 female members, and that the ladies should not be allowed to drop below 11. In addition vacancies should be filled on a 50/50 basis, and odd numbers taken in rotation.

It did not matter, however. Though new members were forthcoming, others resigned due to illness or old age, and there was still not enough interest to make the section properly viable. The mixed matches, so long an underlying feature of the club, ceased in 1996, when the two sections last competed for the Vaux trophies. It was a sad moment. The implication of all of this was that it also had a significant bearing on the financial health of the club.

The 1980's were also characterised by rising costs, as the decline in membership led to belt tightening in the club. Though the ladies had always made some contribution the issue became ever more prominent during the decade. In 1980, for instance the ladies paid £40 to the club to assist with running costs, yet £1000 was spent in 1984 refitting the ladies locker-room, which included the provision of a separate toilet. Discussion took place regarding the ladies paying 50% of the men's fee the same year, but the ladies were naturally reticent about this matter. After some discussion the ladies agreed a figure of £40, while by 1987 this had risen to £75. In the early 1990's this issue was raised again, but 25%was seen as fairer. Nevertheless, since the ladies numbers had declined still further even this seemed disproportionate. The 1992 A.G.M made matters worse as the residential qualification was raised to five years, and by March of 1993 David Ashurst queried whether this new rule applied to the ladies. No particular answer was forthcoming, but by 1994 they were donating £10 per member for the purpose of running costs. It was all a sad saga of decline, with no clear outcome in view.

In 1998 the membership stood perilously at six, and it is difficult to say if a renaissance is at hand. Nevertheless hope still exists, and those that are left continue to enjoy their golf regardless of the numbers remaining. When one looks at the contribution the ladies have made over the decades it would be a shame if the only remaining Artisan ladies section became just a footnote in the long history of golf at Lindrick.

CHAPTER 21
TEAM MATCHES 1945-1998

Team matches had been an integral part of the club calendar in the pre-war years. One look at the fixture list for 1936 shows how many matches were played, and how important they were. Ideal for galvanising team spirit, the matches also had the advantage of fostering inter-club ties, resulting in strong friendships and bonds between the participants.

The post-war period tells a different story though. Between about 1947 and 1960 the situation remained largely the same. Regular matches were played twice annually with Lindrick, but matches with Welbeck were dropped, as during the war the army had taken over the grounds and used it as a base and a training centre for tanks. Thus other clubs were played which included Rushcliffe, Ogden (Halifax) and Renishaw Park, but by the middle of the 1960's even this had run its course.

By the 1970's the club was left with only its twice-annual match with the Parent Club, and the newly introduced match with Serlby Park, which was also played home and away. There was also a match played against Lindrick ladies, while in the 1980's a match was also played against South Yorkshire Police. Nevertheless, these matches were played with much vigour, and today still remain highly competi-

INTER-CLUB MATCHES

Apr.	25	Lindrick G.C.
May	21	Welbeck at Welbeck
	27	Retford at Retford
June	11	Welbeck at Lindrick
	22	Tinsley Park, at Tinsley
July	1	Retford at Lindrick
	6	Tinsley Park, at Lindrick
	13	Beauchief at Lindrick
	20	Beauchief at Beauchief
Oct.	24	Lindrick G.C.

Mansfield yet to arrange

May 30, "Telegraph" Trophy at Hillsborough
July 18, "Telegraph" Cup at Abbeydale

Club Matches 1936.
Owned by Jack Lyon

tive. In this, some things never change.

1947 saw the golf affairs of the club re-organised and back to normal after the war, and this naturally included team games. At this point the individual club competitions were still few- it was only towards the end of the 1950's that new club trophies were introduced- so there was plenty of room in the calendar to arrange club matches. Apart from the usual games the Artisans played against the greenkeepers on 1st July and away to Beauchief on the 29th July, while the committee agreed "we approach the East Midland Ltd for conveyance". The matches were still also very popular and at least one home and away fixture was played each month, while in addition, due to the demand, half strength matches were played on a Thursday, and regarded as second team matches.

Though the matches tendered to promote great team spirit, there were from time to time a few problems to sort out. These centred on players agreeing to play, but not finding a substitute when they subsequently discovered they had other commitments. Indeed, there is one example where a non-member at the time- Eric Taylor- was co-opted by virtue of the fact that he was stood at Woodsetts crossroads when the team assembled, and found itself to be short of a man! The Committee, after lengthy discussion, decided to change the rules governing team matches, so that each member was responsible for paying their share of the expenses, unless they could find a suitable substitute. Any failure to honour these obligations would render the offending member to seek re-election of his membership the following season.

Catering of these matches followed the usual pattern, and has been described in other chapters, but great pride was taken in this part of the day, and appropriate arrangements were always made. In 1948, for instance, the Artisans entertained Bulwell Artisans at the end of August. A cold lunch was provided at Blagg's cafe in Shireoaks at 3/6d a head, while Ellis Colton and his mother arranged tea. However, sometimes the matches were not self-financing, and the deficiencies were sometimes quite large. For example, in 1950 there were losses of £2-7-6d against Tankersley, and £5-12-0d against Bulwell. It was clear that such a situation could not continue, so much so that the Committee stated that "all team matches should pay for themselves, and not require subsidising from club funds."

Towards the middle of the 1950's interest in these contests started to wane. Indeed, in 1955 only two matches and an outing were arranged as a result. There were a number of reasons for this. Firstly, as said, the members started to lose interest, secondly, golf was becoming very popular and the times at which the Artisans traditionally played these matches was now being increasingly required by the Parent Club for their own events. Thirdly, there was a change in the way golf competitions were being organised. Slowly clubs could see the benefit of organising open events, which not only brought their courses in to greater use, but also had the added advantage of bringing in increased revenues. Lastly, Artisan clubs were on the decline. This was particularly so in the 1960's and 1970's when Retford, Renishaw, Bulwell and Rushcliffe all closed. Nevertheless, attempts were made to maintain the spirit of these competitions. Tinsley Park Golf Club asked in 1961 if the match, which the two clubs had traditionally played, could be renewed, while in 1967 Rushcliffe asked the Artisans to play them on the occasion of the Lindrick Invitation Day when the course was closed. As the 1960's drew to a close matches were just being played against Retford, Renishaw Park, and Rushcliffe, but once where they were played twice a year now it was every other year. The respite was short however, and soon these clubs were to be no more. Roy Kipling, writing in the Artisan Golfer magazine in April 1967, summarised the demise by saying that:

"Members seem reluctant to play mid-week, away games are impossible, competitions are favoured [at home] on Saturday's, and Sunday evening seems to have its drawbacks too."

The change in playing conditions in the late 1970's simply confirmed the problem. Tinsley periodically requested a match, but although the Artisans were willing, it was no longer possible to extend them the courtesy of the course, thus the idea came to nothing. Even the idea of playing the match at Breadsall Priory near Derby didn't get off the ground. The same was true with Redcar Artisans. This idea came about due to the fact that the 1981 Northern Tournament was played in Cleveland for the first time. Little came of the idea, even when Pannal Artisans at Harrogate, suggested that a triangular competition should be played between the Artisans from

Pannal, Redcar and Lindrick in 1990.

Yet one match was to survive this decline. This was the contest against Serlby Park Golf Club. The origin of this match was in 1972, and stemmed from a Lindrick member- Eddie Park, who had in the past been a member of Serlby. In the first match the Artisans won at home, but lost away. Overall the Artisans have had the upper hand, but the tight tree lined course, complete with its pheasants and peacocks, has been difficult to master. In the first few years of the match there was nothing to play for other than pride, but in 1984 George Douglas, a well-respected member and past captain, donated a shield for annual competition which has been played for since that time.

By the same token the match played against the Lindrick ladies also lacked a trophy until 1988 when Eric Taylor, the Artisan Match Secretary, donated a glass bowl to give the contest added spice. Highly enjoyable, the hardest part of the match has been the horse trading between the two sides on the number of shots to be given. Over the last twenty-five years or so the match has swung backwards and forwards. During the late 1970's and 1980's the Artisans had the upper hand, but during the 1990's it has been the turn of the Lindrick Ladies, who have won five times. Nevertheless, the real winner has been the forging of good relationships between the clubs.

But the match against Lindrick Golf Club has been, and still remains; the most competed for of all. A previous chapter has told how in the early years the Parent Club tendered to win, but that during the 1930's the Artisans won every year bar one. After the war the same pattern continued, and although written evidence is limited for the 1950's, recollections suggest the Artisans won on most occasions. Nevertheless, the teams were always very strong. In 1965 Lindrick could boast in their team former Walker Cup player Gordon Huddy, as well as David Livingston, a past holder of the Yorkshire Amateur Championship. Pedigree though was insufficient in itself, as professional Jack Jacobs and Norman Tyson defeated them.

In 1966 a big change occurred in the twice-annual match. Jack Jacobs had, in 1965; taken on as one of his assistants a young man called Neil Bray. Tragedy struck though when he was killed in a road accident, and to mark his memory his parents suggested some sort of competition should be played. The question was discussed with the Lindrick Captain Peter Roberts, who in turn discussed the idea with the Artisans. There had never been a trophy for the match against Lindrick, and this seemed like an ideal opportunity, though in sad circumstances, to inaugurate one. After a little debate the Artisans accepted the proposal and the Neil Bray Trophy, a large silver tray, came in to existence.

Since its inception the Artisans have had the best of the matches, and it was not until 1971 that the Parent club recorded their first win. However, in the early 1980's the nature of the match changed. A suggestion was made that it should be played over handicap, and after some debate this was accepted. The result of this seemed to even up the contest as of the next eighteen matches Lindrick won nine of them. Indeed, in the spring match of 1983 the Artisans had lost four out of the last five encounters. In the main the matches were still closely contested, as in 1984 when the Artisans lost six matches to five- when a five at the last would have been good enough to win the game! However, the result was turned around in the autumn when the Artisans did enough to win overall that year.

By the 1990's the contest had evened up again, when the Artisans won six times out of seven from 1991. In the autumn match of 1993 the Artisans won by sixteen matches to one, and Derek Waterhouse, who scored a hole in one, capped the day. 1994 however, was the odd year during this period, as the Artisans lost by twelve matches to two and with it the Neil Bray Trophy. Kevin Hazlehurst, course manager and Artisan Captain, commented wryly that he had thoroughly enjoyed his year of office by "emptying the trophy cabinet", as the matches against the Police and Serlby Park were also lost!

Meanwhile the 1980's saw the introduction of an event played against South Yorkshire Police. Though not classified as an official match this "event", as designated by the committee, has proved very popular. Played both home and away the Artisans have triumphed most times, but it has also paid dividends by helping to keep on the right side of the law! In 1992 it was decided to legitimise the contest by having a trophy to play for, and competition for places is hotly contested.

Though the above matches can, by and large, be considered as official contests there have been other team competitions that the Artisans have participated in. The Whitbread Three Man Team Event, for instance, has provided good grazing for the Artisans. In 1983 a team consisting of Ken Widdison, Brian Dinsdale, and David Locke took the title at Worksop Golf Club, but perhaps the biggest team event is that which is played on the cliff top course at Flamborough near Bridlington.

Whitbread Three Man Team Event 1983. Winning team of Ken Widdison, David Locke, and Brian Dinsdale.
Owned by Ken Widdison.

This event played in early September has seen the Artisans compete for over thirty years, and it is quite interesting how this came about. Frank Stothard, a stalwart member and champion barber, worked in Sheffield, where by chance he met a man called Norman Hemming. Norman, a school master and Sheffield businessman, was also a member of Flamborough, asked Frank if the Artisans would like to send a team to their inter-club competition. Though Frank was unable to make the decision himself, the committee was delighted to accept. So began a connection that lasts to the present day.

Consisting of teams of four, most of the Yorkshire club's are represented, and many clubs actually send several teams to the event. The Artisans have competed every year since 1966, but have only been successful once in the main event when the team of Jack Clarkson, Jack Stocks, Vic and Derek Singleton won in terrific gales in 1975. In the afternoon a two-man team event is played over a shortened course, and in 1996, after thirty years of trying, Eric Taylor and his partner Mick Atkinson won the better-ball competition with 29 points. Yet many players have been lulled in to a false sense of security at Flamborough when they have seen the open spaces and short holes, but the course has nearly always won, because even on a fine day the wind can wreak havoc on the smoothest of swings.

Another event that has attracted interest over many years has been the British Legion organised competitions. For many years after the war men such as Colin Taylor, Arnold Knowles, and Doug Allen, to name but just a few, have taken part in these competitions, both at an individual and team level. In 1964, for instance, Colin Taylor won the individual prize while a team won the combined event.

Though not as important in terms of numbers as before the war, team matches still remain an integral part of the club's calendar, and there is no reason to believe that this will change. There is, of course, no likelihood of the numbers increasing again, but those that remain not only produce enjoyable entertainment, they also forge better links and understandings between the club's. Ultimately, it is these relationships which are at stake and will, undoubtedly, be protected at all costs- because it is on them, that the future of the club lays.

CHAPTER 22
GRAPHITE SHAFTS, BIG BERTHA, AND THE MODERN GAME
1980-1998

At the beginning of the century, when the Artisans had virtually no clubs to speak of, they were by the 1980's; kited out with some of the best equipment that money could buy. Wooden shafts had given way to steel, and now graphite and carbon were leading the way in to the next millennium. But this was not all. The wooden club was now rapidly being replaced by metal, as improved distance and accuracy made their purchase a compelling attraction. In addition, golf balls could fly further than ever, making some of the older courses out of date. Times had certainly changed.

Indeed, much the same could be said for the Artisans. By 1980 the club had reached a crossroads, and no one was sure where the chosen road would lead. Nevertheless, the Artisans had to make the most of it, and from a golfing point of view it was as rich as ever. A new generation of players had come to the fore, and over the next eighteen years men such as David Locke, Roger Whitfield, Roger Merrick, David Rowett, and Mark Merrick were to leave their impression. In support, were the redoubtable Eric Taylor, Ken Widdison, Derek Waterhouse, and Arnold Knowles. In-fact, the period was characterised by the success of the older players. As the club had progressed the membership had aged, and young blood, due to the restrictions, was not coming through as in the past. Thus, as local industries declined, such as coal and steel, so the senior members found they had more and more leisure time on their hands. This they put to good use.

More new club trophies came through during the 1980'and 1990's. The early 1980's saw the first of these with the introduction of the Joe Mee Trophy. Joe, who had been a member since the 1920's, believed the game had changed out of all recognition to when he first started. His idea was to have a competition where the members could use only five clubs and a putter and each player would have to improvise to achieve the best score. In a similar vein came the Silver Birch Trophy that was donated by Terry Lowe, a supporter of the club for many years. In this case it was three clubs and a putter, but the principal was the same. However, after a few years it was decided to abandon this idea, and it is now played for with a full set. In 1985 David Ashurst decided that he would donate a trophy for the most improved youngster. But it was realised that it would be better if it was the most improved player over 20 handicap instead, as young players were few and far between at this time. Also at this time a trophy was given to the club from the Rich family. Though no one is certain exactly how old it is, it is believed to be the first cup ever played for. Not played for now it sits in the trophy cabinet in the clubhouse, a further reminder of the clubs long history.

Towards the end of the 1980's more trophies appeared. Frank Stothard, whose father Jack was the first Secretary had died, and his son wanted to perpetuate the name in the club by donating a trophy. This was accepted gratefully. 1991 saw the Lindrick Golf Club's own centenary, and to mark this they donated a trophy to be played for annually. 1992 saw the sad death of George Merrick; youngest of the three golfing brothers, he was active to the end. George, apart from being a good golfer, and a committed Artisan, was also known for his caddying prowess. In the 60's and 70's he had caddied for Roy Summers, while in later years he kept Tony Maycock on the straight and narrow. Not content with that he also caddied for Kathy Imrie, during the British Ladies Open in 1988. But in his last years he began to caddy for the assistant professional at Lindrick Chris Gray. The partnership had such a lasting effect on Chris, that after George died he decided to donate a trophy in his memory. In 1996 another long serving member had died. Roy Rowett, a member since the early 1930's, past captain, and universally popular, was honoured by the club when they accepted his family's wish that a competition be played in his name. In October of 1996 this was accepted.

During the 1980's pairs competitions were very popular. For example the Daily Mail sponsored their own competition, and several groups of players have competed over the years. For many years Eric Taylor and George Inman represented the club, while in 1980 Ken Widdison and Clive Betts just failed to reach the final stages of the competition

It was also the time of some extraordinary individual performances as well. Spurred on by Alan Dexter's effort in the 1979 Ford competition, other members picked up where he left off. Ken Widdison qualified for the Bob Hope Classic at Moor Park in 1982. Ken, always one for the big occasion, played very well and finished in a creditable fourth place. In the 1984 Ford competition Roy Rowett, aged nearly 70, won the qualifier with a score of 7 under par, beating off the challenges of Ron Tweed and Roger Whitfield who finished second on 6 under par!

Two years later Gerald Locke reached the finals of the Cathay Pacific at Tewkesbury Golf and Country Club when he shot a net 62 to win. The same year veteran Arnold Knowles also qualified for the regional final of the Clerical and Medical Insurance Veterans competition at Moortown Golf Club at Leeds with 37 points. On September 11th Arnold arrived at Moortown with his good friend, and caddy for the day, Roy Rowett. Not surprisingly, he was very nervous, and for the first few holes could hardly play at all. Roy, not accustomed to such a lacklustre performance, took charge of the situation and encouraged his charge to evaluate what he had come for, by saying, "Have we come here to poke at the ball, or to hit it?" Suitably rebuked, Arnold played the round of his life to win the tournament, and with it a reproduction grass driver of 1841. In addition, a place in the national final was secured, which was played at the Jack Nicklaus designed St Mellion golf course in Devon. Unfortunately Arnold could not repeat his earlier success.

The Artisan National Association had never played a tournament at Lindrick, but in 1986 Tony Everett, the National Secretary, enquired whether the Sir William Carr Memorial Trophy could be staged. This was duly agreed to and the competition took place on the 25th September as 36-hole stableford. Although there was some rain in the afternoon, conditions were generally good and Brian Dinsdale came fourth with 73 points, while the experienced Ken Widdison finished in fifth place with 72 points.

Captain's Day and Invitation Day continued in the same manner as in the recent past. The 1981 Invitation Day was significant because the family partnership of Frank Stothard, who by this time was in to his 70's, and his grandson, who was just 13, triumphed with 47 points. But the men to beat throughout the whole period were David Locke and Roger Merrick. David's first Captains Day victory came in 1982, while the following year he and his partner took Invitation Day. In 1987 he was to win once more. Roger on the other hand won Captains Day three times since 1987. Indeed, Roger won the Captains Day Trophy back to back, which would surely have pleased the late Harry Goacher, whose daughter donated the trophy on the death of her mother in 1986.

Invitation Day has also brought many distinguished guests to the club over the years. John "Maurice" Jacobs played in 1971, but in 1988 a fourteen-year-old boy by the name of Lee Westwood played in Captains Day. Though everyone who knew him hoped he would become a good player, no one knew he was going to play in the Ryder Cup and be one of the best players in the world by the time he was 24. Equally, in 1991 Bob Woolley played in and won Invitation Day with Willie Young, the former Arsenal and Scotland defender.

Captains Day 1988. 14 year old Lee Westwood with Lindrick assistant Darren Panks, and David Locke.
Owned by Lindrick Artisans Golf Club.

Of course these special days required all the help that could be mustered, and as ever the lady members, wives and helpers assisted with the catering. But others have also helped down the years. Joe Mee, Harold Brewer, Colin Taylor and Ellis Colton have done starting duties, David Spencer, an ardent former member, has run the putting competition, while Henry Knight and Clive Betts have taken care of the "Halfway House". Indeed, in 1994 Ellis Colton, Doug Inman, Roy Rowett, and Colin Taylor all played the first hole before the first match went out, in the same fashion that the American Masters tournament is started every year. Yet not everything has been plain sailing.

On Captains Day 1995, the tent that was used as the "Halfway House" was stolen from the back of the 11th green. The cost of reimbursement was £115, but by Invitation Day, the Captain, Roger Whitfield, had been given a new tent as a gift for use on suitable occasions.

With such a vast array of trophies now to play for it is possible for most members to realistically have a chance of winning something throughout the season. Once, where a trophy required two or more rounds to play now every week as its own competition, but good play is still required to take these events. Inevitably, the best players in the club who play consistently well all year tend to do the best, but at least others now have more of a chance than in the past. This must be a good thing, so long as standards are not allowed to decline, but the traditionally competitive Artisans are unlikely to let this happen.

CHAPTER 23
CLUB MATTERS 1970-1998

In 1970 Ted Heath and the Conservative Party were in Government, whilst in fashion, flares and long hair were both in vogue. In sport England were losing to West Germany in the World Cup, and South Africa were banned from international cricket. The Artisans, as always, took all of this in their stride. Though much was to change over the next twenty-eight years, the fundamentals, such as the officials of the club, remained largely the same.

Indeed, they were the same as they had been in 1953, with Jack Clarkson as Secretary, Roy Kipling as Match Secretary, and Arnold Knowles as Treasurer. However, in 1974 there was to be a change to this happy balance, when Ellis Colton replaced Arnold Knowles as Treasurer. Ellis was to perform this important job for the next ten years, when Kevan Roe held the position for the following two years.

Due to unforeseen circumstances there was no natural successor, as had been the case in the past, so as a result David Ashurst reluctantly took the role. David, a stalwart supporter of the club, held the office for several years, and as time went by grew in to the position, performing his duties with distinction, until Richard Tweed replaced him in 1993.

The Match Secretary remained unchanged until 1978, when Roy Kipling stepped

Jack Clarkson, Honarary Secretary 1930-1978.
_{Owned by Lindrick Artisans Golf Club.}

down to take up the Secretary's position. For the next two years Brian Dinsdale held the post, but in 1981 Eric Taylor took on the task of managing the new handicap system, a job that he has performed with great distinction since then.

Without doubt however, the biggest change came in 1978, when Jack Clarkson stepped down as Secretary. No one should underestimate the contribution he made, not just to Artisan golf at Lindrick, but also the movement as a whole. He had become Secretary for the first time in 1930, but due to personal reasons stepped down at the end of the year. At the end of 1931 he returned to the district, and regained his position as Secretary, which he was to hold without a break until 1978. Coupled to this he was Chairman of the Northern Section of the Artisan Golfers Association from the early 1950's to 1979. Peter Ellis, writing in the Artisan Golfer in 1966 describes in some detail Jack Clarkson's boundless energy. Not only was he interested in golf, but he was also an active football referee, involved with the British Legion, a poultry keeper, a keen gardener, whilst also a grower of prize chrysanthemum's. Roy Kipling's tribute was succinct and simple when he said:

"Those who have worked with him- which includes two generations of my family- can never forget his efforts. He [was] a man never afraid to listen to new ideas and never afraid to express an opinion."

Having stepped down retirement would have been the expected path for most people, but not for Jack. He was immediately elected Vice-Captain and was club Captain for 1980 at the age of 72. He was though, an ill man, and three years later he died. No greater tribute can be made to "Mr Artisan Golf" than when on news of his death Lindrick Golf Club flew their flag at half-mast as a mark of respect.

When Jack had stepped down as Secretary the natural choice as successor was Roy Kipling. An official since 1953 there was no lack of experience, but it was a difficult act to follow. Nevertheless, Roy did the job his way for the next nineteen years. Indeed, Roy's tenure was through the most difficult years the club had faced, and quoting his namesake, Rudyard Kipling, at the 1997 A.G.M Roy said, "If you can keep your head whilst all about are losing theirs...[then] you'll be a Man my son!" At the end of the year Roy had completed forty-five years of continual service as a club official, and it was time for a new man to take up the challenges of the 21st Century. Terry Mellars, a relatively new member and past Captain, stepped forward to fill the role, and usher the club in to the next millennium. As ever there were matters to attend to, and none more so than the issue of members fees.

Subscriptions, always a bone of contention, rose dramatically between 1970 and 1998. The introduction of the 10% levy to Lindrick Golf Club in 1971 was cause for some alarm. Roy Kipling, writing in the Artisan Golfer, expressed the Committees concerns, when he said:

"The fear is that the genuine Artisan will find the fee too high, and be lost to the club and game. Whilst replacements are ready and available, due to the growth of our villages, the next few years could well bring many problems."

In 1972 the full men's fee was £9.50, while for those under eighteen it was £5. Senior citizens paid £3. By 1980 the subscription had increased to £22, as rising costs had forced prices up on the one hand, while on the other the membership was starting to decline in line with the wishes of the parent club. In 1980 male membership stood at 64, down six on the previous maximum. In addition the number of non-playing members was reduced, so that over the following years there was less revenue coming in to the club. Though this was bad enough, there was another issue that was upper-most in the minds of the committee, when they said:

"Although the increases were substantial, it was felt that it was necessary to look to the future, in view of the average age of the membership, and the present level of costs needed to maintain the premises."

Indeed, in early 1977 the Secretary had conducted a demographic survey that showed that out of the 70 male members 24 were of pensionable age. This was clearly a concern, and the trend only worsened during the 1980's as more and more of the members came of pensionable age. Subscriptions during the 1980's increased steadily, so that by 1988 it had risen to £27.50, with £37.50 being donated to Lindrick Golf Club. Indeed, as the membership fell the burden became ever higher, which was made worse in the early 1990's.

In 1993 a letter was received from the Parent Club informing the

Artisans that the donation would have to increase from 10% to 15% to meet ever increasing costs. Though this was clearly unpalatable, it was accepted reluctantly at a Special AGM. The club subscription before the Lindrick donation was now £40, while by 1997 this had increased to £54, with £106 being payable to the Parent Club. Though the cost of membership had increased, the figure still represented excellent value for money on one of the best courses in the country.

Other costs were incurred in 1974 when the clubhouse was slightly modified to meet fire regulations. Much of the clubs' alterations had taken place in the 1950's and early 60's, but new regulations meant that a fire door, as a secondary means of escape, had to be added. In addition, emergency lighting was required, as were fire extinguishers and training on their use was also a requirement. More importantly occupancy was to be limited to fifty-six at any one time. This was quite a problem, so the decision was taken to extend the clubhouse at the rear, making it flush with the gable end. By putting the fire door in this part of the building and removing the committee room the occupancy could be increased. A small sub-committee consisting of Eric Taylor, George Inman, Norman Tyson, Jack Stocks, and Jack Clarkson was formed to consider the issues. Time was of the essence, however.

In previous years the Kiveton Park Rural District Council had been approached to survey the site. Now though, Rotherham Borough Council, from April 1974, was replacing this authority, as the ruling board on these matters. Fortunately, everything went to plan, and the work was commenced in good time to meet the deadline. The total cost of the alteration was £360, with an additional cost of £97.35 required for electrical work, which was undertaken by Terry Lowe in conjunction with David Ashurst.

Meanwhile, the introduction of V.A.T in 1973 was also a cause for some concern. There was uncertainty as to whether it should be included on the donation to the Parent Club, but after consulting an accountant it was agreed that the club must register for V.A.T, and change its bookkeeping methods accordingly. By the mid 1980's the issue largely went away. This was because the club's turnover was not high enough to meet the registration ceiling, which over the years had increased greater than the income. This was a blessing in disguise during the difficult 1980's.

Unfortunately, by the late 1980's another problem was brewing. A change in the rating system meant a radical change in the way clubs were charged. For the Artisans the increase was dramatic. In 1990 a major review had taken place in business rates in England and Wales, and guidelines suggested that for golf clubs this should be 7 1/2 times the present rateable value. Unfortunately for the Artisans this included the whole golf course and not just the the clubhouse. The question was immediately discussed with the valuation officers, but it was very difficult for them to understand that in effect the Artisans were "tenants". However, after some further discussion the club managed to get a 25% reduction, but in 1995 the value seemed to have been added back as the the increase was almost 80% compared to about 50% for similar premises, such as church halls and working mens clubs. Clearly this was a problem and the matter was taken up with the Parent Club who inturn passed the matter to their valuers Lambert, Smith and Hampton. At the end of 1998 the matter was still unresolved, but upon investigation was a common problem across the country. Nevertheless, the rateable value had increased from £1900 to £3400 in the space of only a few years, something which the Artisans could have done without.

Meanwhile, on a lighter note, the annual Dinner and Prize Presentation, which had been held for many years at the Co-operative Society restaurant in Worksop, was changed to the Masonic Hall where it was to remain until 1996. The event had become very popular, and as a result it was not uncommon for over 150 people to attend the evening. At the same time however, there was also a change in the entertainment that was being provided. Gone were the days where entertainers were employed, or the Artisans did the entertainment themselves: now it was the age of the discotheque, with instant tunes for any occasion. Indeed, in 1974 the cost of the dinner was just £1.50, per person and the hire of a disco was a mere £15. Many of the older members mourned the passing of the old days, but sad though it was, it was also probably inevitable. Perhaps more importantly it was popular, and in 1972 a profit of £22.42 was made. By 1975 this had risen to £34, while in 1977 some 171 dinners were served at £2.10 per head, and a profit of £75.54 was achieved. All of this was in stark contrast to the losses that were made in the early post war period!

During the 1980's the Dinner was at full steam, and much of its success was due to the work done by Norman Tyson who was on the entertainment's committee. In-fact, in recognition of his hard work over many years the General Committee agreed a letter of thanks should be sent recording the fact. However, it was not a one-man show. Both Simon and Richard Tweed, keen Artisans from an early age, had volunteered to run the raffle at the 1982 event producing a profit in excess of £20. The two brothers continued to run the raffle for many years, and even in 1998 Simon was still to be found issuing the tickets with as much enthusiasm as in the past, while at the same time he had taken over Norman's role in organising the event some years previously. Guest speakers were occasionally invited to the event, none more famous than the Artisans good friend John "Maurice" Jacobs in 1982, while the previous year Lindrick member, and Captain of the R & A, Hugh Neil, was the Artisans special guest.

By the early 1990's though, the Dinner's popularity had begun to wane, as the number of members and guests declined. This trend continued until a low was reached in 1996 when only 61 members and guests were present. What the future holds is uncertain, but what was clear was that some re-invention was required to sustain it in to the next century.

John "Maurice" Jacobs presents Brian Dinsdale with the Whitbread Trophy at the 1982 dinner.
Owned by Lindrick Artisans Golf Club.

Another area of concern was that relating to the number of cards each member had to complete to retain membership. The 1935 A.G.M stipulated that the minimum required were three cards, and this remained the same until 1973 when it was officially dropped. However, no official handicap could be awarded until three cards were returned. Very little was heard about this again until the late 1980's when the matter was brought to the A.G.M in 1988. By a close vote, the resolution that three cards must be returned was defeated by 17 votes to 15. By this time it was clear that for some members it was difficult to play in competitions, particularly those who worked at weekends, and since playing competitions on a different day other than the official match day was no longer allowed, it was even harder. In addition, many members simply wanted to play for recreation, and as the population of the club was becoming older, so this trend continued. Furthermore, the 1979 agreement with the Parent Club required less golf to be played, so in an indirect way, if some members did not complete three competition cards then it was of some assistance.

Fortunately, not everything was this involved. The Artisans, for example, had always been very generous in the past when it came to donating money to charity, and much work was done during this period for different organisations. For instance, a great deal was done to help suffers of muscular dystrophy, which was prompted by a member's son being diagnosed with the disease. Special events were held on numerous occasions, one instance being two charity casino nights held in the clubhouse where £367 was raised. Lady member Iris Hall, and also area representative for the charity, was ecstatic at the outcome when she said in a letter to the Secretary:

"I would like to convey my sincere appreciation to the committee and members, for the use of the clubhouse during 1988 for the fund raising events for the Muscular Dystrophy Research Group. As you will have no doubt noted...we raised a total of £367.36- no mean feat for a small club. The money has now been forwarded to Head- quarters, and I eagerly await their reply. My thanks to all concerned."

Over many years money was also raised for the Cancer Research Society. In 1981, Mrs Kath Byrne, a lady member for several years, had died from the disease, and as a result it was decided to donate £10 to the charity. In addition, £25 was donated to the Royal Hallamshire Hospital in 1983 to help buy a body scanner. Further money was raised over the years; for example £55 was raised in 1990, by playing a specific competition during the season.

On a lighter note the club licence was renewed in 1974, for which some work was needed regarding emergency lighting and exits (as described earlier), and successfully re-applied for in 1984 and 1994. This led to other facilities being added. A television was introduced in 1978, which proved very useful for watching World Cup matches, while in 1984 a Pool Table was purchased which has been equally popular. Indeed, in its first month it took nearly £47, an amazing figure when the table only cost £350!

Artisan Members 1996 with Captain Kevan Roe and Vice Captain David Locke front centre.
Owned by Kevan Roe.

In essence, much has happened down the years, but for all the challenges the club had been faced with much progress had been made. In-fact, in 1997, as new Labour set forth on its bold programme of reform, one is left to wonder what new challenges face the Artisans in the next century.

CONCLUSION
THE MILLENNIUM AND BEYOND

There is no doubt that the Artisans could not have envisaged where the generosity of the Sheffield and District Golf Club at the beginning of the century would lead. Where it has led, through each successive generation, is to a point where the club is well established and respected, not just in the broader Artisan family, but also in the Sheffield and wider golfing area.

This respect, of course, has been built on strong foundations, and the present club owes a debt of gratitude to their forebears who built up the structure and organisation of the club in the early years. Without this strength it is unlikely that the present club would be as it today. Of equal importance has been the support of the Parent Club. Parent Club is exactly the right adjective to use here. George Denton, a distinguished member of the Sheffield and District Golf Club, and long serving President of the Artisans, ensured that its offspring grew and developed carefully over the years. Men such as Jack Stothard, Sam Herrington, and Tom Neal all experienced greatly from his guiding hand

In adolescence, Jack Ridgway steered the club to new heights, and under the helm of Jack Clarkson more progress was made- this was particularly so in the '50's and '60's when the clubhouse was rebuilt and extensively modernised. From a golfing point of view it was also a highpoint- including the staging of the Artisan Northern Section Tournament and the wins achieved by Bill Randall, Colin Taylor, and Roy Kipling.

Middle age, if we continue with the analogy, has brought some problems; in particular those associated with reducing membership levels and increased playing restrictions. Yet one thing tends to stand out; that is the club's ability to move with times and re-define fresh objectives. Pragmatic and responsible could almost be the club's motto, but either way it is most apt.

The Artisans have also been shapers, not just followers. It was of course the pioneering spirit of men like Doug Allen and Colin Taylor who established links with the Irish Artisans, which has resulted in the Irish not only coming to Lindrick, but also in establishing an international match between the two national associations. In many ways this might be regarded as Lindrick Artisans greatest achievement.

Though the senior positions in the club have been held by a relatively small group of people, the members have participated in the running of the club, whether on the committee, or when requested for special events, such as during the staging of professional tournaments. This speaks volumes about the Artisans- in that there is a clear commitment to the cause, regardless of the inconveniences.

Now a new century beckons. What does it hold for the Artisans? It is difficult to say with any precision, but one fundamental is vital to continued success- and that is to move with the times. The past will tell us plenty, but we should not dwell there. We should use the past to guide us in the future, by learning both from our mistakes and our successes. Perhaps the single biggest challenge in the immediate future is what fate will become of the ladies section? It would be a sad day indeed if the ladies were to close due to lack of interest and an acceptable method of introducing new members must be found that will encourage competitive golf amongst the members.

Recent work on the clubhouse has brought its standards in to the 21st century, the task now is to ensure that it is progressively enhanced, and that the work done by James Gowans and Jack Clarkson is not allowed to falter. It seems unlikely this will be the case. Nevertheless we should guard against any complacency.

The demands on those responsible for running any organisation or club are always great. The Artisans have always relied upon enthusiastic volunteers to hold the senior posts, and committee positions. Due to the likelihood of continual changes to both working and social patterns there will be the strong possibility that there will be more changes than in the past and each member will need to ask more closely what contribution they can offer.

The Artisan in the next century is going to be a very different person to that in the last. Far more sophisticated than before, the cloth cap and bicycle clip image will be gone forever, and be replaced by the mobile phone and the personal computer. Times change and only the Artisans of the future will be able to tell us how successful we have been in managing that change. It is to them that the club belongs.

APPENDICES

Lindrick Artisans Golf Club Presidents 1912-1999

1912-1928 George Denton
1928-1933 Douglas C Leng
1933-1946 Tom Sorby
1946-1949 Geoffrey M Gullick
1949-1962 Jack Ridgway
1962-1964 Edward A Barker
1964-1968 Jimmy S Ridges
1968-1973 Stephen Wild
1973-1976 Sir Wilton Lee
1976-1979 W H M Smith
1979-1983 John Biggin
1983-1987 Peter Roberts
1987-1990 A McTurk Cook
1990-1992 Tony Maycock
1992-1997 Dougal Rae
1997-   Derek Hepworth

Lindrick Artisans Captains

Year	Captain	Year	Captain
1899 - 1911	Unknown	1960	J.Singleton
1912	A.Taylor	1961	R.Kipling
1913	A.Taylor	1962	D.V.Allen
1914	A.Taylor	1963	S.Inman
1915 - 1923	Unknown	1964	A.Knowles
1924	A.Hargreaves	1965	W.Randall
1925	H.Goacher	1966	G.Merrick
1926	A.Hargreaves	1967	R.Rowett
1927	A.Hargreaves	1968	J.Lyon
1928	R.O.Spencer	1969	H.Brewer
1929	R.O.Spencer	1970	K.Widdison
1930	R.O.Spencer	1971	G.Robinson
1931	R.O.Spencer	1972	E.Colton
1932	E.V.Parkinson	1973	E.Taylor
1933	H.Goacher	1974	J.Stocks
1934	E.V.Parkinson	1975	A.Taylor
1935	H.Goacher	1976	C.Widdison
1936	H.Goacher	1977	B.Dinsdale
1937	H.Goacher	1978	G.Inman
1938	H.Goacher	1979	N.Tyson
1939	H.Goacher	1980	J.Clarkson
1940	F.Ayrton	1981	G.Douglas
1941	F.Ayrton	1982	D.Allen
1942 - 1944	Non elected	1983	E.Johnson
1945	A.Cawkwell	1984	E.Colton
1946	R.Ketley	1985	D.Ashurst
1947	F.Stothard	1986	R.Tweed
1948	A.Cawkwell	1987	C.Straker
1949	J.Mee	1988	K.Spencer
1950	G.Herrington	1989	R.Merrick
1951	H.Goacher	1990	T.Byrne
1952	H.Pollard	1991	M.Hall
1953	O.Clarkson	1992	R.Woolley
1954	H.Merrick	1993	T.Mellars
1955	H.Bedford	1994	K.Hazlehurst
1956	C.Taylor	1995	R.Whitfield
1957	W.Hall	1996	K.Roe
1958	J.Clarkson	1997	D.Locke
1959	T.Widdison	1998	I.Hunt
		1999	R.E.Tweed

Club Officials 1912-1998
Honorary Secretary
1912   Jack Stothard
1913 - 1918   Not Known
1919 - 1921   James Gowans
1922 - 1923   William Merrick
1924 - 1930   Tom Neal
1931 - 1978   Jack F Clarkson
In 1932 Jack temporarily relinquished the position to Arnold Cawkwell for one year.
1979 - 1997   Roy Kipling
1998 - to present Terry Mellars

Honorary Treasurer
1912 - 1947   Sam Herrington
1948 - 1952   Harry Goacher
1953 - 1973   Arnold Knowles
1974 - 1984   Ellis Colton
1985 - 1986   Kevan Roe
1987 - 1994   David Ashurst
1995 - 1998   Richard Tweed
1999 - to present Simon A Tweed

Honorary Match Secretary
1912 - 1923   Not Known
1924   R.O.Spencer
1925   R.Owen
1926   R.O.Spencer
1927 - 1929   Harry Goacher
1930   Ernest Mappin
1931 - 1934   George Herrington
1935 - 1946   Leonard Kipling
1947 - 1949   George Herrington
1950   Ellis Colton
1951 - 1952   Arnold Knowles
1953 - 1978   Roy Kipling
1979 - 1980   Brian S Dinsdale
1981 - to present Eric Taylor

Major Trophy Winners 1946 to 1998

Year	Rose Bowl	Leng Cup	Kayser Cup	Challenge Cup	Foursomes
1946	K.Rowett	A.Spencer	A.Spencer	A.Spencer	H.Merrick / S.Colton
1947	J.Clarkson	J.Clarkson	J.Hall	A.Spencer	A.Spencer / J.Waterhouse
1948	J.Clarkson	R.Kipling	P.Allen	J.Waterhouse	N.Tyson / E.Colton
1949	L.Kipling	O.Clarkson	A.Taylor	R.Rowett	J.Mee / H.Pollard
1950	D.Inman	R.Kipling	W.Randall	J.Hall	D.Inman / R.Rowett
1951	R.Rowett	G.Spencer	J.Merrick	N.Tyson	G.Cawkwell / A.Cawkwell
1952	R.Rowett	A.Knowles	J.Hall	J.Waterhouse	J.Waterhouse / R.Ketley
1953	G.Colton	G.Merrick	A.Knowles	W.Randall	D.Inman / R.Rowett
1954	H.Brewer	N.Tyson	G.Dinsdale	D.Allen	D.Allen / G.Dinsdale
1955	O.Clarkson	F.Stothard	R.Kipling	R.Rowett	J.Hall / K.Widdison
1956	J.Merrick	G.Druary	N.Tyson	L.Morris	J.Hall / K.Widdison
1957	J.Clarkson	J.Palmer	G.Druary	J.Merrick	N.Tyson / D.Allen
1958	G.Harrison	D.Waterhouse	W.Randall	K.Widdison	K.Widdison / J.Palmer
1959	J.Waterhouse	L.Morris	P.Allen	N.Tyson	O.Clarkson / F.Stothard
1960	C.Cocking	T.Dinsdale	W.Randall	W.Randall	T.Dinsdale / P.Allen
1961	F.Stothard	J.Waterhouse	G.Robinson	N.Tyson	K.Widdison / J.Waterhouse
1962	V.Stocks	A.Taylor	W.Randall	R.Rowett	O.Clarkson / F.Stothard
1963	G.Merrick	C.Betts	E.Blagg	C.Betts	G.Dinsdale / T.Dinsdale
1964	J.Stocks	C.Taylor	G.Robinson	R.Rowett	K.Widdison / E.Blagg
1965	A.Taylor	F.Stothard	R.Rowett	E.Taylor	R.Kipling / C.Widdison

Flat Caps and Bicycle Clips

Year	Rose Bowl	Leng Cup	Kayser Cup	Challenge Cup	Foursomes
1966	R.Rowett	K.Widdison	D.Allen	R.Merrick	W.Randall G.Swift
1967	J.Stocks	W.Colton	N.Tyson	K.Widdison	W.Randall G.Swift
1968	V.Stocks	G.Inman	W.Randall	K.Widdison	G.Dinsdale T.Dinsdale
1969	A.Taylor	T.Dinsdale	D.Waterhouse	K.Herrington	E.Taylor H.Merrick
1970	C.Betts	T.Dinsdale	M.Rowett	C.Betts	N.Tyson W.Colton
1971	O.Clarkson	N.Tyson	E.Taylor	E.Taylor	J.Waterhouse D.Waterhouse
1972	J.Inman	M.Rowett	E.Taylor	E.Taylor	N.Tyson W.Colton
1973	G.Merrick	D.Waterhouse	D.Waterhouse	C.Betts	O.Clarkson F.Stothard
1974	J.D.Blagg	R.Rowett	L.Morris	R.Rowett	N.Tyson G.Herrington
1975	K.Rowett	G.Merrick	J.A.Taylor	E.Taylor	R.Rowett D.Allen
1976	D.Waterhouse	L.Morris	E.Colton	K.Widdison	K.Widdison C.Widdison
1977	I.Lilley	I.Lilley	K.Widdison	N.Tyson	N.Tyson E.Taylor
1978	D.Waterhouse	C.Betts	D.Allen	B.S.Dinsdale	B.S.Dinsdale G.Inman
1979	A.Dexter	N.Tyson	A.Dexter	A.Taylor	N.Tyson E.Taylor
1980	A.Dexter	C.Betts	R.Rowett	R.Rowett	R.Rowett D.Allen
1981	E.Taylor	J.D.Blagg	C.Betts	G.Robinson	R.Rowett D.V.Allen
1982	E.Taylor	R.Rowett	N.Tyson	B.S.Dinsdale	C.Betts R.Merrick
1983	C.Betts	G.Merrick	R.Whitfield	K.Widdison	T.Dinsdale D.Waterhouse
1984	R.Whitfield	G.Inman	R.Woolley	R.Whitfield	A.Dexter C.Straker
1985	G.Locke	E.Taylor	T.Dinsdale	B.S.Dinsdale	J.D.Blagg G.Locke
1986	A.Knowles	K.Spencer	G.Inman	J.D.Blagg	J.D.Blagg G.Locke

Year					
1987	D.Waterhouse	K.Roe	D.Waterhouse	C.Straker	G.Inman / R.Whitfield
1988	K.Widdison	K.Widdison	E.Taylor	A.Taylor	K.Widdison / R.Merrick
1989	D.Harrison	R.Whitfield	T.Mellars	R.Merrick	G.Knight / K.Hazelhurst
1990	A.Taylor	R.Whitfield	G.Inman	G.Inman	D.Locke / A.Mellars
1991	D.Waterhouse	K.Roe	G.Knight	G.Inman	I.Hunt / R.Tweed
1992	I.Hunt	D.Rowett	M.Merrick	E.Taylor	D.Locke / I.Waterhouse
1993	T.Dinsdale	R.Tweed	D.Locke	R.Whitfield	A.Dexter / R.Merrick
1994	E.Taylor	A.Mellars	D.Waterhouse	M.Rowett	D.Waterhouse / G.Locke
1995	K.Widdison	I.Hunt	I.Hunt	D.Rowett	I.Hunt / T.Dinsdale
1996	E.Taylor	K.Roe	E.Taylor	R.Merrick	R.Tweed / R.Buckley
1997	M.Rowett	D.Waterhouse	R.Whitfield	M.Allen	K.Hazelhurst / R.Merrick
1998	K.Roe	R.Whitfield	R.Merrick	C.Colton	C.Colton / K.Widdison

Other Trophy Winners 1970 to 1998

Year	Denton Cup	Hallam Trophy	Harrison Trophy	Spencer Trophy	Shireoks Plate	Captains Cup	Barker Trophies
1970	C.Betts	D.Waterhouse	E.Colton	C.Betts	J.Mee	R.Rowett	E.Colton / A.Taylor
1971	C.Colton	G.Robinson	E.Colton	F.Blackwell	C.Colton	H.Merrick	B.Dinsdale / R.Merrick
1972	G.Inman	R.Rowett	E.Taylor	M.Rowett	J.Inman	H.Merrick	G.Inman / E.Taylor
1973	A.Taylor	C.Colton	L.Morris	O.Clarkson	J.Stocks	F.Stothard	A.Knowles / J.Mee
1974	C.Betts	R.Kipling	G.Inman	K.Rowett	J.Blagg	R.Kipling	H.Merrick / C.Colton
1975	K.Rowett	J.Lyon	K.Widdison	K.Rowett	V.Singleton	R.Rowett	E.Taylor / G.Inman

Flat Caps and Bicycle Clips

Year	Denton Cup	Hallam Trophy	Harrison Trophy	Spencer Trophy	Shireoks Plate	Captains Cup	Barker Trophies
1976	K.Widdison	O.Clarkson	A.Mellars	D.Allen	M.Oliver	J.Singleton	R.Merrick B.Dinsdale
1977	I.Lilley	K.Widdison	K.Widdison	K.Widdison	I.Lilley	R.Rowett	J.Mee M.Oliver
1978	G.Locke	J.Taylor	K.Widdison	G.Locke	G.Locke	K.Widdison	J.Stocks D.Singleton
1979	A.Dexter	K.Widdison	A.Dexter	O.Clarkson	A.Dexter	A.Taylor	D.Singleton V.Singleton
1980	G.Taylor	C.Betts	C.Straker	G.Taylor	J.Stocks	R.Rowett	E.Colton E.Johnson
1981	K.Widdison	K.Widdison	G.Taylor	D.Waterhouse	E.Johnson	G.Robinson	A.Spencer J.Stocks
1982	C.Betts	R.Rowett	K.Widdison	J.Blagg	R.Whitfield	G.Merrick	C.Colton T.Byrne
1983	K.Widdison	R.Whitfield	R.Kipling	P.Jones	R.Whitfield	E.Taylor	N.Tyson H.Brewer
1984	J.Blagg	J.Blagg	C.Colton	J.Blagg	R.Whitfield	G.Inman	R.Rowett M.Rowett
1985	T.Dinsdale	G.Inman	H.Straker	A.Taylor	R.Tweed	G.Merrick	R.Rowett A.Knowles
1986	D.Waterhouse	R.Wooley	J.Stocks	M.Hall	J.Stocks	K.Widdison	E.Taylor G.Inman
1987	E.Taylor	D.Locke	D.Ashurst	E.Taylor	M.Rowett	D.Ashurst	H.Straker R.Whitfield
1988	G.Locke	H.Straker	N.Tyson	R.Merrick	G.Knight	N.Tyson	G.Knight R.Merrick
1989	I.Waterhouse	H.Straker	A.Knowles	A.Mellars	A.Knowles	N.Tyson	E.Taylor T.Dinsdale
1990	D.Rowett	I.Hunt	I.Waterhouse	D.Allen	R.Merrick	K.Widdison	E.Taylor T.Dinsdale
1991	D.Allen	R.Merrick	R.Tweed	D.Locke	G.Inman	D.Ashurst	K.Spencer M.Allen
1992	A.Taylor	G.Hutchinson	N.Tyson	K.Roe	R.Kipling	E.Taylor	G.Locke D.Locke
1993	R.Tweed	D.Waterhouse	I.Hunt	G.Hutchinson		G.Locke	M.Hall D.& I Waterhouse
1994	E.Taylor	K.Widdison	I.Hunt	T.Mellars	K.Widdison	R.Merrick	E.Taylor G.Inman
1995	D.Waterhouse	K.Widdison	R.Whitfield	G.West	R.Merrick	R.Merrick	K.Hazelhurst C.Betts
1996	A.Smalley	R.Tweed	D.Rowett	G.West	A.Taylor	A.Taylor	G.Locke D.Locke

148

Flat Caps and Bicycle Clips

Year							
1997	K.Hazlehurst	K.Spencer	R.Whitfield	A.Smalley	K.Hazlehurst	K.Widdison	I.Hunt / M.Hall
1998	D.Rowett	G.West	D.Rowett	I.Waterhouse	E.Taylor	T.Byrne	R.Merrick / G.Knight

Other Trophy Winners 1977-1998

Year	Davenport	Whitbread	H Merrick	Mee	Silver Birch	Captains Day
1977	-	-	I.Lilley	-	-	-
1978	-	-	G.Locke	-	-	-
1979	-	-	R.G.Tweed	-	-	-
1980	-	-	G.Swift	-	-	-
1981	-	-	C.Betts	-	-	-
1982	-	-	M.Oliver	-	-	-
1983	-	-	C.Straker	-	-	-
1984	K.Widdison	D.Locke	J.D.Blagg	K.Widdison	M.Rowett	-
1985	R.Rowett	K.widdison	D.Locke	G.Merrick	G.Merrick	-
1986	R.Merrick	D.Locke	H.Straker	D.Ashurst	K.Widdison	-
1987	M.Hall	A.Dexter	D.Waterhouse	R.Rowett	D.Ashurst	R.Merrick
1988	R.Rowett	A.Taylor	G.Knight	D.Locke	A.Mellars	R.Merrick
1989	G.Inman	G.Locke	A.Knowles	N.Tyson	G.Inman	R.G.Tweed
1990	R.E.Tweed	C.Straker	K.Roe	M.Rowett	R.Merrick	A.Taylor
1991	K.Roe	R.Whitfield	K.Roe	E.Taylor	R.Woolley	D.Waterhouse
1992	E.Taylor	T.Mellars	D.Locke	D.Locke	D.Locke	D.Ashurst
1993	R.Merrick	D.Rowett	D.Waterhouse	K.Widdison	E.Taylor	T.Dinsdale
1994	A.Mellars	A.Mellars	A.Mellars	D.Waterhouse	M.Merrick	M.Allen
1995	D.Rowett	G.Locke	G.West	A.Smalley	G.Inman	K.Widdison
1996	A.Mellars	T.Mellars	G.West	T.Mellars	J.Spencer	D.Ashurst
1997	M.Atkinson	M.Allen	G.West	J.Spencer	A.Mellars	R.Whifield
1998	R.E.Tweed	G.Knight	K.Roe	I.Hunt	M.Atkinson	R.Merrick

Other Trophy Winners 1987-1998

Year	G.Merrick	Stothard	Ashurst	Memento	Rowett
1987	-	-	M.Hall	-	-
1988	-	-	A.Knowles	-	-
1989	-	-	D.Harrison	-	-
1990	-	I.Hunt	R.G.Tweed	-	-
1991	D.Locke	M.Allen	G.Hutchinson	-	-
1992	A.Mellars	M.Rowett	M.Allen	D.Rowett	-
1993	D.Locke	M.Allen	M.Allen	K.Widdison	-
1994	G.Knight	M.Hall	G.West	D.Waterhouse	
1995	M.Merrick	E.Taylor	J.Spencer	D.Allen	-
1996	I.Waterhouse	I.Hunt	K.Roe	K.Roe	-
1997	D.Locke	R.E.Tweed	R.E.Tweed	R.Merrick	M.Atkinson

Flat Caps and Bicycle Clips

1998   R.E.Tweed   G.West   G.West   G.West   A.Smalley

Artisan Tournament (Northern Section) 1945 - 1998

News of the World Challenge Cup 1928

1952 W.Randall
1958 C.J.Taylor
1964 R.Kipling
1971 G.Robinson
1973 L.W.Morris

Sir Lindsay Parkinson Rose Bowl 1937

1952 W.Randall
1961 J.Merrick
1962 R.Kipling
1965 G.Robinson
1966 W.Randall
1971 O.Clarkson
1975 R.Kipling
1976 D.V.Allen

News of the World Cup 1964

1970 J.Mee

W.J.Gardner Cup 1964

1968 V.Stocks

Harry Jackson and Frank Brookhouse Trophy 1996

1998 G.West

Scratch Cup 1948 Presented by the late West Cheshire A.G.C

1972 C.L.Betts

COPY OF
THE FIRST ANNUAL CIRCULAR ISSUED PRIOR TO THE 1946 A. G. M

Woodsetts Artisans Golf Club

Dear member,
It is with great joy that I convey to all members of the Woodsetts Artisans Golf Club the hearty greetings of the Chairman and Officers of the Artisan Golfers Association on the return of a long awaited state of Peace after the trials and inconveniences which each one of us has experienced during the past six years, we may now look forward to brighter days with more frequent opportunities for resorting to our favourite recreation.

Although most of our members are employed in heavy industries and have been working to their maximum capacity, from the playing point of view, season 1945 has been very disappointing. Anyhow it is very gratifying to know that we have carried on in a very modest way, and I would like to appeal to all members, to renew their efforts in 1946 to get the club resuscitated. I am proudly aware that the depleted playing strength of the club is due in no small measure to many of the boys being in uniform, and it is my earnest hope, that they will experience no delay in exchanging their war weapons for their golf clubs.

It was the fervent desire of "The News of the World" that the Artisans should have played their Annual Tournament in 1945, and it is with great reluctance that the idea had to be abandoned. Firstly no suitable course was available, and there was the problem of feeding, accommodation, travel etc., and it was agreed that it would not be fully representative, that the idea was finally shelved. Anyhow to offset this disappointment, the "News of the World" has expressed a hope that that our 1946 Victory and Re-Union Tournament will produce a record entry, and I ask all interested members to give early consideration.

The Annual General Meeting of the Association will be held in London sometime in January when a large and representative gathering will make the arrangements for the past war campaign.

It is interesting to note that after five years, contact has been made again with the Channel Island golfers, who appear to be making very light of their deprivations.

Just a few words about our own affairs. The competitions were arranged during the past season, the entries proved so disappointing no further competitions were ventured. Some members made the weather the excuse, while others (would be golfers) had no balls. Let us hope the latter problem will be resolved before the 1946 season begins, so that there are no excuses for not joining competitions.

Members of the Buxton & High Peak and Halifax Artisans and certain members of Beauchief and Tinsley Park have already expressed a desire to play team matches in 1946. It very doubtful whether we will be in position to do any catering for such like events, but I sincerely hope that we will be able to make a start with team matches. Our biggest problem is the dilapidated state of the clubroom, without which makes it very difficult, and not very inviting to arrange anything. Anyhow we welcome suggestions from any member to help put the "house" in order.

Appending below is a copy balance sheet for season 1945.

Income		Expenditure	
Balance B/F from 1944	1-5-7 1/2	Trophy and fire insurance	8-3
Subscriptions	12-5-0	Hire of school for meeting	2-6
New members	18-9	Receipt book	1-6
Ladies Section 3rd Part Ins	9-6		
24 members O.H.M.S @ 5/	6-0-0	Third Party Insurance	1-13-9
Sheffield Union	10-6	J. Unsworth's Prize 1940	5-0
		Secretary's Postage acct.	3-4 1/2
Balance in hand	5-14-0		
Total	£14-18-10 1/2		£14-18-10 1/2

J. F. Clarkson
Honorary Secretary

BIBLIOGRAPHY

Books

A history of Lindrick Golf Club, 1891-1979.J.Arthur Colver.Sheffield 1980

The Observers Book of Golf.Tom Scott.London 1975.

Minutes

Minutes of Lindrick Artisans Golf Club 1912-1998.

Minutes of Lindrick Golf Club 1899-1936.

Magazines and Newspaper Articles

The Artisan Golfer 1947-1998.

Golf Illustrated June-October 1957

The Worksop Guardian Newspaper

The Sheffield Telegraph Newspaper

Photographs

Present and former members have kindly donated all photographs, which have been acknowledged in the text. Some of these may have copyright status, please therefore accept my apologies in advance for any infringements that may have occurred.

Contributions

I am indebted to the following for giving their time freely to help in the completion of this work.

Clive Betts, Bessie Brewer, Frank Brookhouse Secretary of the Artisan Golfers Association (Northern Section), Ellis Colton, Alan Dexter, Trevor Dinsdale, Tony Everett National Secretary of the Artisan Golfers Association, Mick and Iris Hall, Cynthia and Ken Herrington, Margie Herrington, The Irish contingent (including Peter Archbold and Tom Kinch), George Inman, Jack Jacobs, Roy Kipling, Graham Knight, Arnold Knowles, Jack Lyon, Roger Merrick, Terry Mellars, Jessie Rowett, Kevan Roe, Kitty Spencer, Eva Spencer, Alan Taylor, Colin Taylor, Eric Taylor, Norman Tyson, Anne Tweed, Roger Whitfield, Ken Widdison and last but not least, Graham West.

INDEX

1961 Licensing Act 66

A

A. Clarkson 36
A. E. Turnell 16
A. Goacher 4
A. Hargreaves 18
A. Richard Westerman 35
A. S. Jackson 55
A.G.M. 14
Abbeydale 26, 102
AGM 23, 134
Alan Dexter 78, 146
Alan Spencer
    4, 5, 31, 44, 49, 54, 57, 60
Alan Taylor 4, 6, 50, 86, 143
Alec Betts 17
Alf Randall 26
Alice Morris 100, 110, 112, 113, 116
Alison Nicholas 108
Annual honorarium 52, 62, 89
Anston 65
Area Coal Board Trophy 73
Arnold Cawkwell
    5, 21, 34, 35, 39, 40, 73, 143
Arnold Knowles
    4, 61, 62, 63, 71, 76, 82, 125, 126, 128, 131
Arnold Palmer 66, 89
Arnold Taylor 13, 14, 17, 18, 23
Arthur Foulds 46
Arthur Hargreaves 38
Artisan Golfer
    38, 83, 84, 95, 97, 104, 121, 132, 133, 153
Artisan golfer 92
Artisan Golfers Association 3
Artisan Golfers Red Cross Appeal 46
Artisans
    3, 4, 5, 6, 12, 13, 14, 15, 16, 17, 18, 19, 20, 21, 22, 23, 24, 25, 26, 27, 28, 29, 32, 33, 34, 35, 36, 37, 38, 40, 41, 42, 44, 46, 47, 50, 52, 54, 57, 58, 59, 60, 61, 62, 65, 67, 68, 69, 70, 71, 72, 75, 76, 77, 78, 79, 80, 81, 82, 83, 84, 86, 88, 89, 90, 91, 92, 93, 94, 95, 96, 97, 99, 100, 101, 102, 103, 105, 106, 107, 109, 110, 111, 112, 114, 115, 120, 121, 122, 123, 124, 125, 126, 129, 130, 131, 134, 135, 136, 137, 138, 139, 140
Audley Clarkson 36

B

Banning Cup 21, 73
Basil Gray 31
Beauchief 25, 26, 52, 120, 152
Bernard Wragg 24

Bessie Brewer
    100, 110, 112, 113, 114, 115, 116, 154
Bill Farley 96
Bill Randall
    5, 60, 81, 83, 104, 114, 139
Bill Taylor 63
Billy Wade 41
Bob Charles 106
Bob Hope Classic 128
Bob Jacobs 18, 24, 38, 43, 78
Bob Kay 12
Bob Woolley 129
Brian Barnes 107
Brian Dinsdale 72, 107, 124, 128, 132
Brian Waites 107
Brown Bayleys 25
Bulwell 23, 25, 120, 121
Bulwell Artisans 14, 23, 120
Burglary 75
Butchers Arms 13, 19, 41, 77
Buxton 40
Buxton & High Peak 152
Buxton and High Peak 26, 81, 82

C

C. T. Tant 29
Cancer Research Society 137
Captain's Cup 18
Captain's Day 96, 128
Captain's day 71, 96
Cavendish Golf Club 83
Challenge Cup 29, 37, 54, 72, 83
Charles Colton 35
Charlie Colton 5, 34, 35
Charlie Spencer 15
Chauffeurs room 29, 53
Chauffeurs room 39
Chris Gray 127
Christmas Fayre 60, 74, 75
Clement Attlee 61
Clerical and Medical Insurance Veterans 128
Cliff Herrington 5, 20, 21, 37
Clive Betts
    6, 63, 72, 74, 77, 83, 84, 127, 130
Clontarf Golf Club 97
Club Championship 59
Co-operative Society 63, 135
Colin Taylor
    49, 80, 81, 82, 85, 86, 95, 97, 99, 100, 104, 106, 107, 125, 130, 139
Commonside Foursomes 37, 54, 72
Corrine Dibnah 108
Curtis Cup 63, 105
Cynthia Herrington 19

155

D

D-Day 47
D. Goacher 14, 42
Davenport 149
Davenport Trophy 77
David Ashurst 118, 127, 131, 134
David Craven 90
David Lindsay 58
David Livingston 122
David Locke 6, 86, 124, 126, 129, 138
David Rowett 6, 86, 126
David Spencer 64, 130
Dennis Brown 71, 75
Denton Trophy 72, 77, 78
Derek Waterhouse 6, 74, 123, 126
Dernie and Bell 69
Dick Mayer 104
Dinner and Prize Presentation 62
Dinnington 13, 28, 29, 39
Doug Allen
    49, 57, 63, 73, 82, 85, 86, 95, 97, 99, 107, 114, 115, 125, 139
Doug Ford 104
Doug Inman 62, 82, 104, 130
Dougal Rae 106, 142
Douglas Leng 21, 23, 24, 32, 34
Dr P. J. Quigley 36
Duncan McIntosh 90, 94
Dunlop Masters 6, 66, 107

E

E. Sims 54
Earle and Proberts 54
Easter uprising 17
Eaton Hall 36
Ebor handicap 70
Ed Furgol 104
Eddie Park 122
Eddison 18, 19, 25, 33
Edith Bowles 42, 110, 112, 114
Edward Knowles 17
Edwin Eddison 25
Electric light 39, 40
Ellis Colton
    3, 4, 5, 13, 35, 48, 55, 57, 61, 62, 75, 78, 89, 104, 120, 130, 131, 144
Elsham 114, 115
Elvaro Pratt 108
Eric Taylor
    4, 85, 86, 104, 115, 120, 122, 125, 126, 127, 132, 134, 144
Ernest Mappin 26, 34, 37, 41, 144

F

F. H. Price 55
First World War 17, 23, 42
Flamborough 124, 125
Frank Colton 35
Frank Stothard 37, 73, 103, 124, 127, 128
Frank Taylor 5, 18, 20, 21, 24
Fred Hawkins 104
Fred Marsh 70

G

Garforth 112, 113, 114
Gary Player 89
General Strike 20
Geoffrey Gullick 37, 52, 59, 68
George Bowles 12
George Cawkwell 24
George Denton
    5, 12, 13, 14, 15, 21, 24, 34, 42, 72, 139, 142
George Dinsdale 103, 106
George Douglas 122
George Hallam 59
George Herrington
    29, 31, 34, 41, 61, 144
George Hutchinson 108
George Inman
    74, 88, 90, 91, 127, 134, 154
George Merrick
    37, 49, 60, 63, 76, 104, 108, 114, 127
George Robinson
    57, 60, 78, 83, 86, 89, 97, 99
George Spencer 30, 50
Gerald Locke 128
Gerard Kirke Smith 20
Goacher family 19, 42
Golden Ball 62, 63
Goodwin tournament 102
Gordon Huddy 122
Graham West 86, 154
Grand National 70
Great War 20, 42
Growth of the locality 65
Guy Hunt 107
Gwen Steadman
    6, 42, 43, 44, 112, 114
Gwen Swift 111, 112

H

H. Betts 20
H. Crapper 16
Halfway House 77, 130
Hall and Son 69
Hallam Trophy 72, 77, 78, 147
Hallowes Golf Club 55
Harold Brewer 58, 60, 130
Harold Colton 50
Harold Eardley 23, 24, 31, 37
Harold Macmillan 57, 72
Harrison Trophy 59, 78
Harry Bates 56
Harry Bedford 60
Harry Goacher
    4, 5, 15, 18, 19, 23, 28, 35,

39, 40, 44, 58, 61, 69, 70, 129, 144
Harry Kipling   18, 48
Harry Pollard   35, 37
Henry Knight   77, 130
Henry Westby   19
Hillsborough Golf Club   48, 77
Hitler   47, 49
Home Guard   49
Horace Cawkwell   14, 15, 18, 23, 27
Horace Merrick
   5, 33, 34, 35, 41, 56, 63, 78
Hubert Green   107
Hugh Boyle   106
Hugh Neil   136

I

Ian Hunt   86
Ian Lilley   78
Industrial Revolution   10
International match
   95, 96, 97, 108, 140
Invitation Day
   41, 77, 112, 121, 128, 129, 130
Iris Hall
   99, 100, 111, 112, 113, 114, 116, 137, 154

J

J. Allison   11
J. Arthur-Colver   4
J. Cawkwell   11
J. H. Coldwell   24
J. H. Taylor   10, 80
J. Kennedy   56
J. Shone   14
J. Sorby   65
Jack Burke   104
Jack Clarkson
   4, 29, 30, 38, 39, 49, 52, 54,
   60, 61, 63, 66, 67, 68, 70, 74,
   84, 89, 92, 103, 106, 111, 114,
   125, 131, 132, 134, 139, 140
Jack Colton   47, 50
Jack Hall   60, 114
Jack Inman   26, 49, 77
Jack Jacobs
   31, 63, 75, 78, 79, 122, 154
Jack Lyon   77, 78, 154
Jack McGeer   96, 97, 98, 100
Jack Nicklaus   89, 128
Jack Palmer   59, 60, 63, 74, 103
Jack Ridgway
   5, 59, 68, 70, 71, 75, 139, 142
Jack Stocks   67, 125, 134
Jack Stothard
   12, 14, 15, 16, 18, 23, 27, 139, 144
Jackson Brothers   69
James and Harry Scaife   62
James Braid   106
James Brownlow   12, 14, 15, 16

James Gowans
   17, 18, 20, 24, 27, 40, 140, 144
Janet Twibell
   6, 42, 43, 44, 63, 110, 111
Jarvis Allen   12, 14
Jerry and Prince   50
Jessie Rowett   110, 112, 113, 154
Jim Highfield   57
Jim Merrick
   5, 34, 54, 57, 60, 80, 82, 104
Jim Oldale   57
Jim Waterhouse   5, 26, 80, 114
Joan Ashurst   111, 116
Joan Widdison   110, 112, 115, 116
Joe Mee   29, 30, 83, 126, 130
Joe Rylands   98, 99, 100
Joe Twibell   20
John Hooker   96
John "Maurice" Jacobs   76, 106, 136
John Rowbottom   12

K

Kitty Spencer   110, 112, 113
Kathy Imrie   108, 127
Kayser Cup   36, 54, 59, 78, 145
Ken Herrington   20, 72, 73, 154
Ken Widdison
   6, 73, 78, 80, 81, 85, 86,
   107, 108, 110, 114, 124,
   126, 127, 128, 154
Kevin Hazlehurst   123
Kiveton Park Rural District Council
   54, 68, 69, 134

L

Ladies Golf Union   42, 110
Ladies Inter-Club Team Trophy   112
Ladies Open Championship   107, 127
Ladies Open Meeting   43
Ladies section formed   6
Lady Bingham   43
Lady Bingham Cup   43, 111
Lambert, Smith and Hampton   135
Laura Davies   108
Lee Westwood   129
Lees Hall   35, 55
Len Morris   57, 73, 74, 85, 95, 104, 110
Leng Cup
   21, 22, 43, 54, 59, 60, 72, 73, 77, 78, 145
Leonard Kipling
   4, 29, 30, 31, 33, 41, 46, 47, 144
Lily Inman   111, 112, 115
Lindrick   3, 4, 10, 11, 12, 17, 18,
   20, 23, 26, 27, 29, 30, 32, 35, 36,
   40, 43, 44, 48, 49, 52, 55, 56, 58,
   60, 62, 64, 65, 66, 68, 71, 73, 74,
   76, 78, 80, 81, 82, 84, 88, 89, 90,
   91, 92, 93, 94, 95, 96, 97, 98, 99,
   100, 101, 102, 103, 105, 106, 107,

Flat Caps and Bicycle Clips

109, 111, 113, 114, 118, 119, 121, 122, 123, 127, 128, 132, 133, 134, 136, 140, 142
Lindrick Beatles 64
Little Aston 83
Lloyd Merrick 20, 34
Lorraine Hall 100, 116
Luke Seymour 89

M

Maesdu Golf Club 82, 85, 95
Major Sutton. H. Lowe 31
Marchioness of Titchfield Cup 36
Mark Merrick 6, 86, 126
Martini International 107
Michael Carroll 96
Michael Rowett 72, 77
Michael Sinnot 96
Mick Hall 98
Ministry of Works 69
Mobilisation of the Artisans 46
Moortown Golf Club 128
Mrs Kayser 36
Muscular Dystrophy Research Group 137

N

Nancy Merrick 115
Neil Bray Trophy 123
Neil Coles 66, 106
Neville Davenport 77
News Of the World Challenge Cup 81
News of the World Challenge Cup 82, 83, 84, 150
News of the World Challenge cup 85
News of the World Medal 46, 58
Norman Hemming 124
Norman Tyson 5, 33, 35, 49, 55, 57, 58, 75, 107, 122, 134, 136, 154
Northam Artisan G. C. 10
Northern Artisan Tournament 5, 21
Northern Section of the Artisan Golfers Association 4, 37, 132

O

Ogden 52, 110, 119
Oscar Clarkson 37, 39, 57, 77, 83

P

Palaise de Danse 70
Pannal Artisans 121
Pat Kenny 96
Peter Allis 106
Peter Archbold 98, 99, 100, 154
Peter Mills 104
Peter Osborn 71
Peter Thomson 106

Pick 71
Pick, John and Percy 29
Playing conditions 18, 27, 43, 53
Pool Table 138
Presidents Bowl 19, 21, 22, 43
Presidents Cup 15, 19
Presidents Putter 74
Prestbury 22

R

R Edwin Eddison 18
R Harper 84
R. Deizall 41
R. Eddison 33
R. O. Spencer 4, 25, 29, 58, 60
Redcar Artisans 121
Refit of 1998 68
Reg Colton 33, 37
Reg Ketley 18, 20, 23, 24
Renishaw Park 84, 119, 121
Retford 18, 25, 36, 121
Reverend Ramsden 84
Rich family 127
Richard Sparling 55, 58
Richard Tweed 100, 131, 136, 144
Ridgway Arms 71
Robert Owen 17
Roberto de Vicenzo 106
Roger Merrick 6, 63, 72, 85, 126, 129, 154
Roger Whitfield 86, 126, 128, 130, 154
Ron Tweed 128
Rose Bowl 19, 77, 78, 82, 83, 112
Rose bowl 98
Rother Vale 44
Rotherham Golf Club 35
Roy Kipling 3, 4, 6, 38, 47, 57, 62, 67, 71, 80, 82, 83, 85, 86, 89, 103, 104, 121, 131, 132, 133, 139, 144
Roy Rowett 5, 31, 49, 74, 107, 110, 127, 128, 130
Roy Summers 76, 89, 127
Royal Blackheath 10
Royal Insurance Co. Ltd 39
Rushcliffe 115, 119, 121
Ryder Cup 6, 71, 75, 89, 102, 103, 107, 129

S

S. Berisford 55
S. White 19
Sam Herrington 4, 12, 20, 29, 30, 31, 61, 139, 144
Sam Kendrick 84
Sandbeck 13, 17
Second World War 5, 35, 37, 44
Serlby Park 119, 122, 123

158

Sharpe Brothers 41, 62
Shaun Waide 88, 90, 91
Sheffield and District Golf Club 23
Sheffield and District Golf Club
  4, 10, 11, 15, 18, 21, 23,
  25, 27, 31, 32, 38, 39, 43,
  53, 54, 139
Sheffield Telegraph 55, 58, 153
Sheffield Telegraph Cup 35, 55, 58
Sheffield Union 46, 55, 77
Shireoaks 4, 11, 12, 13,
  18, 19, 22, 25, 28, 29, 33,
  50, 53, 59, 62, 65, 70, 74,
  78, 89, 103, 110, 120
Silver Birch Trophy 127
Sir Albert Bingham 29, 37, 43
Sir Harry Lauder 49
Sir Lindsay Parkinson Rose Bowl
  81, 82, 83, 85, 150
Sir Stuart Goodwin 71, 102
Sir William Carr Memorial Trophy 128
Sir Wilton-Lee 65
Smith Cup 20, 22
South Yorkshire Police 119, 123
Southport and Ainsdale Golf Club 48
Spencer Trophy 72, 75, 77, 78, 112
St Leger 70
St Mellion 128
Station Hotel 13, 53, 62
Stephen Wild 142
Subscriptions 133, 152
Subscriptions 14, 62
Sun Alliance Match Play Championship 106
Sun Alliance Matchplay Championship 6

T

Tankersley 115, 120
Ted Highfield 5, 20, 21, 25
Ted Kroll 104
Telegraph Trophy 35, 55
Terrence Gillatt 49
Terry Byrne 86, 100
Terry Lowe 127, 134
Terry Mellars 133, 144
The News Of the World Challenge
  Cup 81
The News of the World Challenge
  Cup 82, 83, 84
The Shield 48
This is Your Life 63
Tinsley 21, 25, 52, 56, 73, 121, 152
Tom Burdell 84
Tom Kinch 98, 99, 100, 154
Tom Neal
  4, 12, 24, 29, 31, 35, 37, 44, 139, 144
Tom Scott 10, 153
Tom Sorby 25, 29, 32, 40, 142
Tommy Bolt 104

Tommy Mappin 40, 41
Tommy "Thunder" Bolt 104
Tommy Widdison 26, 29, 63
Tony Barker 81, 104, 142
Tony Everett 3, 92, 128, 154
Tony Jacklin 106
Tony Maycock 127, 142
Trevor Dinsdale 64, 72, 106, 154
Turnerwood 4, 11, 28, 29, 53, 65

V

Vaux trophies 117
Vic and Derek Singleton 125
Vic Parkinson 26, 29, 34, 39, 41
Vic Stocks 83
Vivian Jacobs 6, 42, 43, 44, 110

W

W H M Smith 142
W.H.M. Smith 71
W.J. Gardner Cup 83
W.J.Gardner Cup 150
Walter Neal 37
Walton Heath 96
Weetabix Ladies Open 107
Welbeck 25, 26, 36, 119
Welbeck Golf Club 14
Wendy Wisburn 108
West Lancs. Golf Club 85
Westward Ho! 10
Wheatley Golf Club 58
Whist nights 70
Whitbread Three Man Team Event 124
Wilf Hall 80
William Colton
  12, 13, 16, 17, 18, 20, 23, 35
William Merrick 21, 27, 39, 144
William Randall 33, 36
Woodbrook Golf Club 96
Woodsetts 4, 11, 13, 15,
  19, 23, 26, 28, 29, 31, 35,
  41, 53, 61, 65, 70, 89, 110, 120, 151
Worksop Golf Club 25
Worksop Golf Club 26, 43, 44, 73, 124
Worksop Guardian
  24, 26, 32, 35, 36, 44, 153
World Matchplay Championship 66

Y

Yorkshire Amateur Championship
  102, 110, 122
Yorkshire Union Championship 15

Thanks To Our Sponsors

Assidoman Sacks (UK)
N&C Pallets
Gascoigne Emballage
O.T. Africa Lines
Beer Seller
John Good and Sons
Linpac
Wilkinsons
Alder Products Ltd
Tiger Tim Products Ltd
Wright Bros.